MARGARET MEAD

A Portrait

Also By Edward Rice

THE PROPHETIC GENERATION

THE MAN IN THE SYCAMORE TREE

MOTHER INDIA'S CHILDREN

TEMPLE OF THE PHALLIC KING

THE FIVE GREAT RELIGIONS

JOHN FRUM HE COME

THE GANGES

JOURNEY TO UPOLU

MARX, ENGELS AND THE WORKERS OF THE WORLD

TEN RELIGIONS OF THE EAST

EASTERN DEFINITIONS

BABYLON, NEXT TO NINEVEH

CITIES OF THE SACRED UNICORN

MARGARET MEAD

A Portrait

by Edward Rice

HARPER & ROW, PUBLISHERS

NEW YORK

Cambridge   London
Hagerstown   Mexico City
Philadelphia   Sao Paolo
San Francisco   Sydney

1817

Library of Congress Cataloging in Publication Data
Rice, Edward.
Margaret Mead

Bibliography: p.
Includes index.
SUMMARY: A biography of Margaret Mead as seen
through her work.
1. Mead, Margaret, 1901–1978—Juvenile literature.
2. Anthropologists—United States—Biography—Juvenile
literature. [1. Mead, Margaret, 1901–1978.
2. Anthropologists] I. Title.
GN21.M36R5 1979   301.2′092′4 [B] [92]   ·76-3827
ISBN 0-06-025001-1
ISBN 0-06-025002-X lib. bdg.

ACKNOWLEDGMENTS

The author gratefully acknowledges permission to excerpt from the following works:
Columbia University Press for *Omaha Secret Societies* by Reo F. Fortune. Copyright 1932.
Reprinted by permission of Columbia University Press.
Doubleday & Company, Inc. for *The Complete Short Stories of Somerset Maugham* and *A
Writer's Notebook* by Somerset Maugham. Reprinted courtesy of Doubleday & Company, Inc.
E. P. Dutton and Routledge & Kegan Paul Ltd. for *Sorcerers of Dobu* by Reo F. Fortune.
Copyright 1932 by E. P. Dutton, renewal 1960 by Reo F. Fortune. Reprinted by permission of
the publishers.
Harper & Row, Publishers, Inc. for scattered excerpts from *Letters from the Field 1925–1975*
by Margaret Mead. Volume Fifty-two of the World Perspective Series edited by Ruth Nanda
Anshen. Copyright © 1977 by Margaret Mead. Reprinted by permission of Harper & Row,
Publishers, Inc.
William Morrow & Company, Inc. for *Blackberry Winter: My Earlier Years* by Margaret Mead.
Copyright © 1972 by Margaret Mead. *Coming of Age in Samoa* by Margaret Mead. Copyright
1928, 1955, 1961 by Margaret Mead. *Growing Up in New Guinea* by Margaret Mead. Copyright
1930, 1958, 1962 by Margaret Mead. *A Way of Seeing* by Margaret Mead and Rhoda Métraux.
Copyright © 1970 by Margaret Mead and Rhoda Métraux. All by permission of William Morrow
& Company, Inc.
The New York Times Company for an article on Margaret Mead by Laurie Johnston, December
16, 1976. Copyright © 1976 by The New York Times Company. Reprinted by permission.
Stanford University Press for *Naven* (2nd ed., 1958) by Gregory Bateson. Reprinted by permis-
sion of Stanford University Press.

Frontispiece: Margaret Mead in Tambunam, New Guinea, 1938. Photo by Gregory Bateson.

To Beth and Cathy

Contents

PART ONE

PART TWO

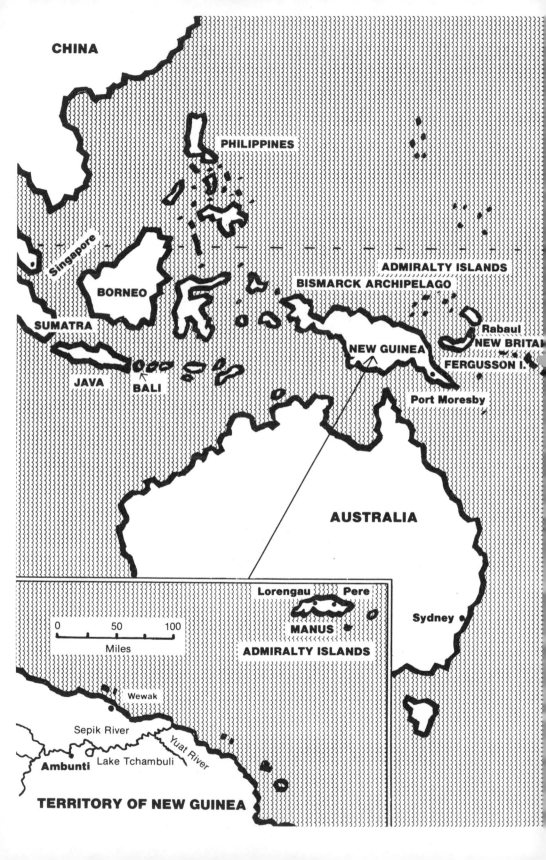

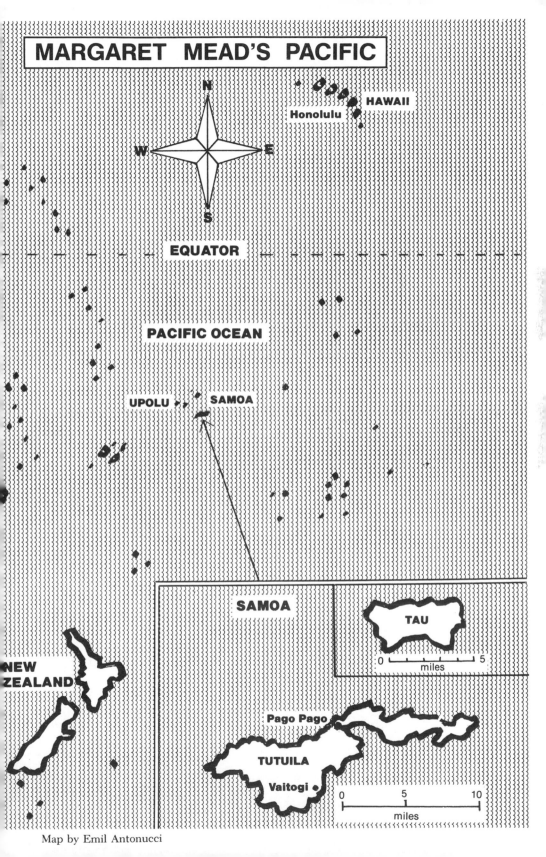

MARGARET MEAD'S PACIFIC

N
W   E
S

HAWAII
Honolulu

EQUATOR

PACIFIC OCEAN

UPOLU   SAMOA

SAMOA

TAU

0   5
miles

NEW ZEALAND

Pago Pago

TUTUILA

Vaitogi

0   5   10
miles

Map by Emil Antonucci

MARGARET MEAD

A Portrait

Introduction

"THE WAY IN WHICH each human infant is transformed into the finished adult, into the complicated individual version of his city and his century is one of the most
fascinating studies open to the curious minded." So wrote
young Margaret Mead after her first field trip to the Manus
island people. The date was 1929.

The same statement might have been applied to Margaret
Mead herself, for her own life—an unusual and exciting
one—was an example of how an infant developed not only
into a "finished adult" but, moreover, into one of the legends
of our age, for she stood bigger than life on our anthropological, sociological and cultural horizons.

Even if Margaret Mead had not gone into professional life
but had remained within the boundaries of her own milieu—
that of the intelligent, well-educated, literate, verbal middle-
class American—she would have been a good example herself
for study by an objective observer of Western culture. Suppose, for example, that one of the so-called "primitive," Stone
Age headhunters of New Guinea, where she had done so
much research, had possessed the same type of anthropological "tools" that she had used in her own studies. Suppose he
had been able to apply her own methods to an analysis of

Margaret Mead. What would he have found? What would he
have made of this slight, self-possessed, energetic woman,
who could arrive out of the unknown, find a house and work
area in a jungle village, quickly learn a foreign tongue and the
customs and traditions of another culture and assert herself
as a human being? What kind of soul-force guided this tiny
woman? What was her myth-dreaming? What ghosts did she
answer to? What was her totem and her clan? Who was her
brother? Did she bring a dowry or was there a bride-purchase
price? How many dogs' teeth or pigs was she worth?

What follows is a reply of sorts to the New Guinea islander,
the biography of an unusual woman, half of whose life had
been spent in faraway places, whose mind could absorb unfamiliar themes and connect the daily life of primitive
cultures—religion, methods of child care, rites of initiation,
marriage and death—directly to the most complex American
way, with its thousands of variations in living, rural, urban
and suburban, and its many ethnic and cultural strains.

Whatever she had studied, obscure cannibal tribes, a
declining Indian reservation, a simple Balinese village, the
rituals, customs, traditions and rebellions of her own people,
Margaret Mead had been able to relate them all into a global
unity. Even in the most primitive society she had often discovered amazing parallels to the American way. She could
compare the easygoing, simply structured adolescence of Samoan girls with the complex, often contradictory choices presented to the teenage American of the same period. And she
had been able to establish direct comparisons between the
Manus, a canoe-culture, trading people of the South Pacific,
who worried incessantly about business and their neighbors'
opinions, and the upwardly mobile, automobile-loving
Americans of the new suburbs of the 1920's.

The Manus were a central theme in Margaret Mead's life.
In 1928 the Manus were a scattered tribal society of some

13,000 people living in offshore stilt houses on a remote island off the northern New Guinea coast. When she left their coral lagoons after six months of study, she had thought she would never see them again.

She had expected that the Manus would become a depressed proletariat. Instead, quite unexpectedly, they joined her in the twentieth century, compressing five thousand years of human development into fifty, the same half century of adult life that Margaret Mead enjoyed after meeting them. In a way they were partners with the people of America in working their way through the twentieth century.

The lives of the Manus and Margaret Mead, a tribe and an individual who had met by chance, became interwoven by historical forces outside everyone's control. Both parties, these Melanesian islanders and the young anthropologist, seized the historical moment.

It is this unifying thread, of Margaret Mead and the Manus, that ties together the diverse themes of this biography, for the Manus became more important to her than her work in any other area, and more significant than the many other important tasks she was to accomplish and the numerous honors she was to gain.

PART ONE

Coming of Age

ONE TORRID DAY IN AUGUST 1925, a slightly built young woman in a cotton dress steps ashore on an island in the South Pacific. It is Margaret Mead, twenty-four, thin, perceptive, aggressive, student of the much neglected science of anthropology. "Travel lightly" several people have advised her. In her scanty baggage she has five more cotton dresses and some simple tools for her work—notebooks, a camera, a portable typewriter. She intends to study a previously ignored field: the ways in which girls in a primitive society—in this case Samoa—grow up. She hopes—expects—that her projected study will shed some light on how this segment of Pacific island culture relatively unaffected by modernization attains maturity. She has already been warned that what has been written about Samoan culture is anything but fresh and uncontaminated by Westernization. But the growing up of young women in Samoa has so far been ignored.

Mead is one of a small group of anthropologists in the United States, a few professionals—who also teach, argue and theorize and engage from time to time in field trips—and some students; there are probably not many more in Europe, and a number of the U.S. anthropologists were born abroad. Anthropology—the study of peoples and their physical, social

3

and cultural characteristics—is, in 1925, a relatively minor subject, almost unrecognized in the academic community. But the anthropologists, like warriors holding some embattled post, are concerned that the ancient, archaic and primitive societies that still exist will disappear soon under the pressures of modernization. Already the metal ax, the nail, the outboard motor and the Gramophone have replaced the stone knife, the peg dowel, the canoe paddle and the tribal chant in many cultures. Plywood and plastic threaten. From one end of the globe to the other the societies that had so interested and intrigued early explorers, traders and missionaries are changing, giving way to the more powerful forces of the industrial nations.

The journey to Samoa was not easy to embark upon. Young Mead had to battle her elders to get started. She had been given permission to undertake the project with some reluctance by her teacher, the noted anthropologist Franz Boas. He worried that she lacked the stamina to endure a harsh life in the tropics remote from Western amenities. "I myself am not very pleased with this idea of her going to the tropics for a long stay," Papa Franz (as he was familiarly called by his students) had written to Ruth Benedict, his assistant, and also a close friend of hers. "Margaret is high-strung and emotional." Yet Boas feared that if Mead didn't make the trip she would become depressed. One of Boas's colleagues, the anthropologist and linguist Edward Sapir (like Boas, German-born), had been quite blunt with her. He told her that she was not strong enough to survive in the field—that she would do better to stay at home and have children as a woman should than to study adolescent girls in the South Pacific.

But subtly defiant and skillfully manipulative, Margaret Mead worked her way around her teachers' fears, and now

she is in Pago Pago, Samoa, about to prove herself far more
resilient than her elders had imagined.

En route to Samoa Mead stops briefly in Honolulu, still an
undeveloped Pacific outpost, a scandalous port of bars, broth-
els, shops, warehouses, slums and factories. Fortified by numerous letters of introduction, she visits friends of friends,
who smooth paths for her. Through them she reaches the
inner circle of the famed Bishop Museum, repository of a
hundred disappearing Pacific cultures, and is able to begin a
study of Marquesan, a tongue related to Samoan. A friend of
a new friend presents her with a hundred small squares of old
torn muslin "to wipe the children's noses." Someone else
recommends always carrying a little pillow and "you can lie
on anything." Practical advice.

Mead meets a part-Samoan family who give her the
names of relatives still at home. It is a felicitous beginning,
and extremely pleasant, she notes. After two enjoyable
weeks ashore, happy in the anticipation of her coming
work, and weighed down with flowered leis of farewell,
she boards the boat for Pago Pago, capital of the Samoan
island of Tutuila.

After an uneventful week at sea, the ship glides past the
fragrant shores of Tutuila, and into the great circular bay at
Pago Pago. It is a wonderful, even awesome sight, a thin strip
of silver beach crowded by the encroaching brush. The bay,
second in size and importance as a naval base only to Pearl
Harbor at Honolulu, is large enough to hold a fleet. Towering
over Pago Pago is Mount Matafao, 2,141 feet high, almost
purple in the heat. Here and there Mead can see the thatched
tops of the Samoan houses, and among the lush tropical green-
ery the simple accents of the white mission churches. But the
effect is spoiled by the constant roar of airplanes overhead

and warships dripping oil into the calm waters.

She is not particularly interested in Pago Pago, but she must stay there while arrangements are made to go to a less developed island for her studies. The heat is oppressive; in fact the entire Samoan archipelago is moist and often unbearably uncomfortable. The rainy season runs from October to March, and coincides with her stay in the islands. The English novelist Somerset Maugham, who had visited Samoa a few years earlier, wrote in his journal, "There is not a breath of air in Pago Pago. It is terribly hot and very rainy. From out of a blue sky you will see heavy grey clouds come floating over the mouth of the harbour, and then the rains fall in torrents." It is the ever-present rain that forms the background of Maugham's famous story about a woman named Sadie Thompson, which was later made into a play (and a movie) called *Rain.*

Mead takes a room in a hotel overlooking the harbor. It is the same hotel in which Maugham had sat for two weeks waiting out a small epidemic of chicken pox that prevented his boat from continuing to another island. Maugham described it in some detail.

> The lodging house. It is a two-storey frame house with verandas on both floors, and it is about five minutes walk from the dock, on the Broad Road, and faces the sea. Below is a store in which are sold canned goods, pork and beans, beef, hamburger steak, canned asparagus, peaches and apricots; and cotton goods, lava-lavas [a kind of sarong], hats, rain-coats and such like. The owner is a half caste with a native wife surrounded by little brown children. The rooms are almost bare of furniture, a poor iron bed with a ragged mosquito-curtain, a rickety chair and a washstand. The rain

rattles down on the corrugated iron roof. No meals are provided.

Such is the setting for her introduction to anthropological work. Because she is a woman, the National Research Council, which is helping to underwrite the costs of her research, has decided she cannot be trusted with her entire grant in advance, and so has insisted on sending it in monthly portions. The mails are slow, get lost. Her first check—for $150—has temporarily disappeared in the languor of Samoa. The hotel costs $28 per week; until she receives her allotment she cannot leave. She must spend six weeks in the lodging house, at times the only occupant, without money to pay her bill. Six "laborious and frustrating weeks" in a kind of tropical house arrest. But she begins to learn Samoan.

The lodging house has added a cook-boy after Maugham's time, a young man called Misfortune—in Samoan, Fa'alavelave. Mead has mixed reactions to Samoan food. "Dreadful" is her first verdict. "Papaya and coconut oil and taro, that tasteless yet individual carbohydrate, serve for taste and the frangipani blossoms with their heavy oppressive odor for smell, mixed on the warm breeze with the odor of slightly fermented overripe bananas" is how she describes her introduction to Samoan cuisine in a letter home. Later she learns to eat and "enjoy" Samoan food, but even after that she can add it was "painfully learned." (And even fifty years after her first field trip she can remark that "Learning to eat the food is harder than learning the language.")

Her letters of introduction get her, through the navy medical department, a Samoan tutor, Pepe, who speaks excellent English. She has an hour a day with Pepe and seven hours a day trying out her accumulating knowledge of Samoan on the children she encounters in her walks.

Another letter of introduction. She meets the governor, "an elderly and disgruntled man."

"I have not learned the language and you will not too," he remarks.

"It is harder to learn languages after one is twenty-seven," she replies.

An incautious remark is her afterthought.

Her money arrives at last, and she is freed from the lodging house and Misfortune's dreadful meals.

A Samoan woman, a member of the family she had met in Honolulu, arranges for her to spend ten days at Vaitogi, a village near Pago Pago. Here Mead stays with the family of a chief. The daughter, Fa'amotu, teaches her Samoan etiquette, the proper things to do and say in various situations according to the circumstances. She learns how to sit on the floor—painful at first, and her legs ache—how to sleep on mats, and how to act during the rituals of meals and ceremonies. She puts away her cotton dresses and wears a lava-lava, the all-purpose unisex garment worn from East Africa to the Pacific. When she bathes under the village shower, in the full sight of staring children, she learns how to slip off the wet lava-lava and put on a dry one without feeling clumsy.

In Vaitogi the food is "wonderful." Two chickens every day for herself, with breadfruit, mangoes, limes, papaya, pineapple, tea, coffee, American-style bread, and fish.

She takes up Samoan dancing, which, she writes home, is not practiced "in a puritan fashion." She probably does not know that Maugham's missionaries—the actual people upon whom he based his story—were "very bitter about the dancing." The natives were crazy about dancing, the missionaries had found. "We made up our minds the first thing to do was to put down the dancing."

On her first field trip—to Samoa—Margaret Mead often goes barefoot and wears a Samoan lavalava. Her companion here is Fa'amotu, who teaches Mead Samoan customs and helps her with the language.

Mead will dance many nights throughout her stay.

Pains in the legs from sitting on the floor and from too much dancing go away. She is rapidly becoming acclimatized. Samoanized. The food in Vaitogi is better. The lessons in Samoan etiquette produce results. Samoan society is highly structured, and rank is important. One behaves a certain way for this person in the hierarchy, that way for another. One must use the correct phrases.

A chief from the neighboring island of Upolu visits the family. After a while he makes an offer which Margaret attempts to put into perspective. But she is able to affirm in her broken Samoan, "marriage" between them would not be fitting due to the difference in their respective ranks. She hopes her Samoan is adequate to the occasion.

Regrets. But the chief adds: "White women have such nice fat legs."

Returning to Pago Pago, with its veneer of Westernization gained from the naval base, Mead hears from her friends that she should do her research in a more "old-fashioned," that is, unspoiled, area. She is offered quarters at the medical post at Tau, an island in Samoa's Manu'a group.

Chief Pharmacist's Mate Edward R. Holt and his wife Ruth give her living space on a verandah at the rear of the dispensary. From here she can see the village. Nearby is a small Samoan house she is to use as a center and office, and where she can talk in private to the Samoan girls. She is in an ideal situation for her work: She has the authority of the government behind her, and can thus maintain the privilege of rank; had she lived with a Samoan family, etiquette would have kept her from talking to the village children. Now, with a Samoan girl as her companion and teacher, she can wander about the village and talk to anyone. Equally important, as she writes home, "I can be in and out of the native homes from early in the morning until late at night and still have a bed to sleep on and wholesome food. . . . The Navy people have canteen privileges."

She goes to work. But immediately she wonders if she is approaching her work properly. She has complained on several occasions that anthropological students learn theory but not practice; no one in the field for the first time truly knows what to do. (One anthropologist's first impression was that "the feet of the natives are large.")

"The truth was," she states, "that I had no idea whether I was using the right methods. What were the right methods? There were no precedents to fall back upon."

In graduate school at Columbia University there had been little information about how to proceed in the field. The student was sent out with very vague notions of what to do once he or she had landed among "his" or "her" people. Mead's teachers had been two of the greats of anthropology, Franz Boas and Ruth Benedict, but sometimes even they had emphasized abstractions more than how to proceed face to face with primitive people of far distant cultures, customs and languages.

With her head crammed full of the highest levels of anthropological concepts but blank about working procedures, Mead takes a commonsense approach. She is in Samoa to learn, and she goes about learning much as her aged grandmother, Martha Adaline Mead, had taught her when she was growing up in small towns in rural New Jersey and Pennsylvania—to go out and observe, listen, ask questions, analyze and write it all down in her notebooks.

Fieldwork, Mead notes about her first trip, is very difficult. One must clear one's head of misconceptions and presuppositions about other cultures and open it up to the flood of new and unexpected information that comes pouring in. A practical approach seems to be the solution.

Accompanied by an ever-changing group of young Samoan

girls, she wanders about, asking questions and checking the questions with other questions. She analyzes each household in three neighboring villages of Manu'a, noting down location, relationship and closeness to other households, rank, wealth, and the age, sex, social standing and marital status of each person in the household. Each child is studied in the context of her own particular environment.

"In the field nothing can be taken for granted," she remarks. Even the fact that people live in houses should be seen as if for the first time. She notes that Samoan houses are round, with a pagodalike roof and open sides—no enclosing wall shuts out the view of the entire village. The floor is made of pebbles, and rolled-up mats are kept for the arrival of visitors. At night a bark-cloth curtain is all that separates the guest from the family. This openness of the Samoan house helps her get a picture of the daily comings and goings of the young people she is working with. Details build up the great picture, and she misses nothing, not even the slightest nuances of gesture and language.

Mead works as long as there are light and people awake to talk to or watch or overhear. But she has other methods, too, of establishing the character of each girl's life. Sometimes she tries standard Western tests in interviews, among them color-naming, completing drawings, interpreting pictures, rote memory of numbers and digit symbol substitution, and word tests. In some of them, especially those involving numbers, the girls do poorly or have no interest; but they excel at words, and often with drawings. She also draws up charts of standard activities, such as gardening, fishing, weaving, making bark cloth, athletics, to learn the girls' understanding of their own culture and its numerous codes and taboos, and fills them in casually as she gathers information about each person.

Her self-taught methods of fieldwork are to produce one of

the most unusual books of anthropological history. Nuances of Samoan life are captured, slight events others might have overlooked. In her hands they show a novelist's touch.

The life of the day begins at dawn, or if the moon has shown until daylight, the shouts of the young men may be heard before dawn from the hillside. Uneasy in the night, populous with ghosts, they shout lustily to one another as they hasten with their work. As the dawn begins to fall among the soft brown roofs and the slender palm trees stand out against a colourless, gleaming sea, lovers slip home from trysts beneath the palm trees or in the shadow of beached canoes, that the light may find each sleeper in his appointed place. Cocks crow, negligently, and a shrill-voiced bird cries from the breadfruit trees. The insistent roar of the reef seems muted to an undertone for the sounds of a waking village. Babies cry, a few short wails before sleepy mothers give them the breast. Restless little children roll out of their sheets and wander drowsily down to the beach to freshen their faces in the sea. Boys, bent upon an early fishing, start collecting their tackle and go to rouse their more laggard companions. Fires are lit, here and there, the white smoke hardly visible against the paleness of the dawn. The whole village, sheeted and frowsy, stirs, rubs its eyes, and stumbles towards the beach. "Talofa!" "Talofa!" "Will the journey start today?" "Is it bonito fishing your lordship is going?" Girls stop to giggle over some ne'er-do-well who escaped during the night from an angry father's pursuit and to venture a shrewd guess that the daughter knew more about his presence than she told. The boy who is taunted by another, who has succeeded him in his sweetheart's favour, grapples with his rival, his foot slipping in the wet sand. From the other

end of the village comes a long drawn-out, piercing wail.
A messenger has just brought word of the death of some
relative in another village. Half-clad, unhurried women,
with babies at their breasts, or astride their hips, pause
in their tale of Losa's outraged departure from her father's house to the greater kindness in the home of her
uncle, to wonder who is dead. Poor relatives whisper
their requests to rich relatives, men make plans to set a
fish trap together, a woman begs a bit of yellow dye from
a kinswoman, and through the village sounds the rhyth-
mic tattoo which calls the young men together. They
gather from all parts of the village, digging sticks in
hand, ready to start inland to the plantation. The older
men set off upon their more lonely occupations, and
each household, reassembled under its peaked roof, settles down to the routine of the morning. Little children,
too hungry to wait for the late breakfast, beg lumps of
cold taro which they munch greedily. Women carry piles
of washing to the sea or to the spring at the far end of
the village, or set off inland after weaving materials. The
older girls go fishing on the reef, or perhaps set themselves to weaving a new set of Venetian blinds.

We are immediately at home in the thatched, circular
houses, at peace under the lazy, swaying palms, engrossed in
the amatory intrigues of the young girls and boys. We see a
life of simplicity and ease that is beyond our experience, yet
the ideal of our dreams. Swimming, fishing, living in the
open, dancing, storytelling, ceremonies, an economy without
the need for money, sexual experimentation—in the 1920's
this is far beyond the hopes of the ordinary Westerner, even
among the young.

But along with this idyll, Mead is careful to point out (but
a point that many readers will ignore), come social responsi-

Margaret Mead begins her Samoan fieldwork in the village of Vaitogi. She stays with a chief named Ufuti, who formally makes her a member of his family. The little boy with Mead is Paulo, also part of the chief's household.

bility and social integration. In her Samoa even the five- and six-year-olds have definite and understood responsibilities, caring for the younger children, learning to plait palm or pandanus leaves, to climb coconut palms, to open coconuts skillfully, and attending to numerous other minor but necessary chores. Boys go through the child-caring stage and then move on to their assigned tasks, helping with the fishing and preparing boats for sea. In their teens the girls will learn the ways of cooking with primitive equipment (stones, bamboo leaves, coconut shells, plaited baskets and carved bowls), and the boys will pick up the techniques of canoe handling, of tending taro roots and coconut trees, transplanting and harvesting. Each boy must take part in communal activities, not slacking or showing too much precocity. He must fit into the larger structure, for individuality is discouraged.

High-strung and frail her professors had thought she might be in the field, yet Mead has accomplished an amazing job. She has worked with sixty-eight girls mainly in the three neighboring villages of one coast of Tau. From time to time she visited four other villages in the Tau archipelago, and she talked to numerous children, young men and adults. Her broad observations about ceremonial usages surrounding birth, adolescence, marriage and death are collected from the entire group, but it is the teenage girl's psychological development that is crucial to her work.

In *Coming of Age in Samoa*, the book that resulted from her trip, her most important discovery is that the storms and tensions of adolescent life in the Western world are not necessarily shared by other peoples. Unlike adolescence in America and Europe, she discovers, Samoan "adolescence represented no period of crisis or stress, but was instead an orderly developing of a set of slowly maturing interests and activities. The girls' minds were perplexed by no conflicts, troubled by no philosophical queries, beset by no remote ambitions. To live as a girl with as many lovers as long as possible and then to marry in one's own village, near one's own relatives, and to have many children, these were uniform and satisfying ambitions."

The idea seems to appeal to a lot of her readers, and her frankness in speaking so plainly about sex and love in Samoa soon make her famous.

Everyone's Favorite

SHE IS A PRECOCIOUS, EAGER, inquisitive child. "There's no one like Margaret," the family says, half in admiration, but at times with a touch of annoyance. Nevertheless, among all the children of Edward and Emily Fogg Mead, Margaret is everyone's favorite.

She is a Sagittarian. An Archer: "someone who goes as far as anyone else and shoots a little farther" is her definition. But as a scientist astrology means nothing to her.

The Meads have five children: Margaret, born in 1901, is the eldest; Richard, the only boy, is two years younger; Katherine dies in infancy in 1906; after her come Elizabeth, born in 1910, and Priscilla, born in 1911.

Edward Mead is a professor at the Wharton School of Finance and Commerce, part of the University of Pennsylvania. He is the author of a number of books about business subjects, and edits a railroad magazine.

Emily Fogg Mead, three years older than her husband, is working on her master's degree in sociology at the time of Margaret's birth. In 1901 it is still unusual for a woman to attend and be graduated from college—at best, many young women go to what is called a finishing school to learn social graces before marriage—and postgraduate education is even

Emily Fogg Mead, 34, and young Margaret, age four. This is the period when Emily Mead is studying Italian-American families in Hammonton, New Jersey. She often takes Margaret on her field trips.

rarer. However, Emily Mead is hard at work on an unusual subject for her master's thesis: Italian immigrant families in the then-rural town of Hammonton in southern New Jersey, not far from Philadelphia.

As a child of three, Margaret accompanies her mother on visits to the immigrants. They are mostly former agricultural workers and slum dwellers who have come to America along with tens of thousands of others in search of opportunities they cannot find in their homelands. The Italian families are warm and open, and they serve as the first introduction in Margaret's education as an anthropologist. She sees that there are other ways of life, other languages, other forms of relationships between families, husbands, wives, children, cousins, uncles and aunts from what she is experiencing in her own academically centered home. One form of living is not necessarily better or worse than another, merely "different." Each way of life, with its unique history, thoughts, culture, customs and religious beliefs, might be strange—"foreign"— to the casual observer, but is nevertheless normal in its own context. A basic lesson that is imprinted early on young Margaret's mind.

Her mother's thesis receives little recognition, Mead notes. It is eventually published as a pamphlet by the United States Government Printing Office. Its value lies in another field: It helps young Margaret in learning how to see other people. Two decades later it will serve as the basis for some of her own studies.

For a while these researches into the lives of the immigrants dominate the Mead household. The family had moved to Hammonton in 1904 in order to be closer to Emily Mead's subjects. The town is an ideal place for raising children. Here the Meads live in an old farmhouse on five acres of land, with blueberry thickets, woods with secret pathways, trees to climb, a barn and an abandoned dinghy planted with flowers.

Part of each year the family returns to Philadelphia so that Professor Mead can be closer to his job. For two winters the Meads live in the city itself, and then in different outlying suburbs, usually among other members of the academic community.

During this period of moving from one home to another, from country to city or suburb, Margaret has but one full term of formal schooling; this on a half-day basis only, much to the envy of her other classmates and the annoyance of teachers. It is an age when truancy laws are not readily observed. Her other terms in school are fragmentary. Most of Margaret's schooling comes from her own family members. But by the time she is nine, young Margaret is led to the mature decision that this hopping about has its disadvantages, for in her first month of fourth grade, she fails at arithmetic—"dismally" is the word she uses. However, by the third month of the term she has made a great discovery: School is a system. From near failure, she rises to a 90 percent grade in arithmetic.

She carries the step further. Not only school but life itself is a system is the conclusion she reaches in later years: A home, a town, a school, a classroom subject, a primitive society—all are "systems" with their parts and pieces to be studied, analyzed and mastered. Life at Hammonton, superficially chaotic, is a system. Most children would have found little in the Meads' moves but a memory of pleasant disorganization. An analytical mind like young Margaret's is needed to see the basis of a lifetime of ordered discipline out of what passes as daily living and learning in the Mead household.

An interesting, powerful figure dominates young Margaret's education: her father's mother, Grandma Martha Adaline Mead, who, more than her mother and father, influences Margaret's life. She lives with the family, a tiny, strong figure with flashing dark eyes and an endless fund of information. As a girl in her mid-teens (she had been born in 1845), she had become a teacher in a local school in Winchester, Ohio, though it was uncommon for so young a woman to teach. When the Civil War ended in 1865, she married a young ex-soldier, Giles Mead, who had just been demobilized. Together, the young couple went to college. Giles Mead became a school superintendent, expert in reorganizing problem schools, and Martha left teaching. But Giles died young, only thirty-nine, leaving Martha Mead with a six-year-old boy, Edward Mead—Margaret's father—to bring up. Martha Mead taught in various schools, or served as principal, until 1900, when Edward Mead, now twenty-six, and Emily Fogg married. Martha then came to live with them. By that time she was fifty-five.

Clearly Grandma Mead, active, decisive, loving, and intelligent—the young Margaret's model and favorite adult—gains both obedience and devotion, not by acting dictatorial but by the simple graciousness of her being. Grandma Mead, says Mead of her grandmother almost seventy years later, "was the most decisive influence of my life. She became my model, when, in later life, I tried to formulate a role for the modern parent."

Easily but effectively Grandma Mead teaches the four Mead children the ways of running a country house. They learn how to tend gardens, raise chickens, cook and can. It is a frontier-type life, close to the land, working with what one grows, finds, makes, not with what one buys.

Grandma Mead is also Margaret's first and most important tutor. She supplies what the school fails to supply: She teaches algebra (in preference to arithmetic, which she curiously believes is injurious to young minds) and botany. She is a moralist in her approach: Every lesson is accompanied by anecdotes meant to illustrate some virtue or positive quality.

"She taught me until I went to high school and even then helped me with my lessons when my teachers were woefully inadequate, as they often were," says Mead. And after each day's formal work, Grandma Mead sends Margaret to the woods and meadows to learn about plants, and explains how to analyze and catalog each specimen. Much of what Margaret learns is to be of value in her approach to fieldwork in later years as an anthropologist and scientist.

Grandma Mead leads Margaret to one of her most important discoveries: "I was always glad I was a girl," she writes in her autobiography, *Blackberry Winter.* Grandma Mead "had no sense at all of having been handicapped by being a woman." In another passage: "I think it was my grandmother who gave me my ease in being a woman." Grandma Mead's stories are liberally sprinkled with accounts of "a fair number of no-account men in each generation and, appropriately, a fair number of women who married the same kind of men."

Mead's other grandmother, her mother's mother, Grandma Elizabeth Bogart Fogg, gets short shrift. A small handsome woman with snapping black eyes, "dutiful but lacklustre with children." A sharp tongue: She calls Margaret "tiresome." No love is lost in Margaret's later memories. At sixteen she gives Grandma Fogg a volume of Guy de Maupassant stories inscribed, "To my wicked little grandmother." "A quality of inconsequential triviality" is her summing up, a verdict which, in *Blackberry Winter,* she stretches to include her own mother and her sister Priscilla. But there must have been some special spirit in Grandma Fogg: In her nineties she ran away from the old age home in which her children had deposited her. Wicked woman!

Margaret's mother Emily is not so broad and open as Grandma Mead. As a young woman, Emily Fogg had been determined and earnest, and at the same time careful and humorless, characteristics she retains in adult life. In growing up, Margaret can see that her mother is not happy about Grandma Mead's favored position in the household ("Mother never ceased to resent the fact that Grandma lived with us"), yet Emily Mead always makes sure that her mother-in-law has the best room in the house.

Emily Mead is altruistic in public causes. She vehemently fights the local political machine, protests the slaughter of birds for decorating hats, opposes the telephone company, Standard Oil and sweat shops. Battles that have not yet been won. But for the people she meets personally, Emily Mead has only gentleness and a radiant welcome.

Emily Mead could be comfortable about life, her daughter remembers: The Mead home is filled with books and papers, and the children are encouraged to participate in the household, not forbidden because they might disarrange things. Margaret's views about her mother are thus mixed with pleasant memories and some criticism.

Blue eyes, golden hair, slight. An old photograph shows Emily Mead as a fine-boned, beautifully vibrant woman with a Mona Lisa smile and bright, intense eyes. Professor Mead, who is a good six feet tall, calls five-foot Emily Mead "Tiny Wife," a name the child Margaret also uses in addressing her mother.

Years later Mead observes that her mother believed life was too serious for little pleasures—she disdained pretty clothes and elaborately dressed hair, since more serious things demanded her time and energy, not only for running the house and raising a family but for various causes and for righting the wrongs done to the downtrodden. Was she too efficient, too committed? In the luxury of the quiet of her last years, after a stroke, Emily Mead confides to her son-in-law Leo Rosten (Priscilla's husband), "Margaret always wanted a little rose-bud mother." At death she is dressed in pale blue and given a bouquet of sweetheart roses.

Margaret's father, Edward Sherwood Mead, occupies an even more ambiguous place on her horizon. The passing of time may have mellowed the harsh views she seems to have held during her growing years. She is never clear whether Dada (who calls her "Punk") is one of those no-account men in the family, for he had too high a position in the university to be slighted, or whether he was a major figure diminished by the fact that he was never so important as he might have been. Or at least, as important as she thought he wanted to be. Nevertheless he stands as a commanding figure, tall, strong, well organized and in control of his universe, with a voice that makes known his wants.

Sixty and seventy years afterward, Margaret Mead can make some biting remarks about her father. One suspects the battles between them were even fiercer than she admits to in public. In her own old age we can see that she resented some of his characteristics—"He thought he could buy anything with money," Mead remarked shortly before her death—and she hints that he was unfaithful to her mother, and that he was far from honest in his dealings with Mead on the question of her going to college. Yet in the end she tries to be fair and objective about him, and makes allowances for the problems he experienced. But—"I resented furiously what I regarded as his entirely arbitrary intrusions into our lives . . . represented by his very occasional acts of discipline. . . . In general, however, he left the supervision of his daughters to my mother and concentrated, instead, on worrying about and overprotecting his son."

It is through her father that she learns about the world of academia, the university world where men jockey over intellectual standing and scholarly credit quite as ruthlessly as

Margaret Mead's father, Edward Sherwood Mead, as a young professor at the Wharton School, where he teaches economics. He also edits a railroad magazine and experiments with various business projects.

men in business do for power, adopting ruses and stratagems to ensure their own positions. Such knowledge is to be helpful when she enters university life herself and has to learn how to steer a course between conflicting demands and to maintain her own interests in the face of pressures to conform to others.

Professor Mead teaches economics and his business courses are among the best at Wharton Graduate School, but practical business interests him too. He is an editor of *Railway World* (at a time when American railroads were a major economic force). He is also the author of several books, among them *The Ebb and Flow of Investment Values*, *The Careful Investor*, *Corporation Finance*, *Trust Finance*, and *The Story of Gold*. The latter work seems to have been his daughter's favorite, for of all his books it is the only one she describes in detail in her autobiography. She notes how he began with an abstract interest in the economy of gold, and then, as he became more absorbed in his subject, the book developed into an account of the entire use of the metal, from mining to its practical possibilities.

Professor Mead is an inveterate tinkerer with the business process, attempting to turn abstract theories into economic realities. On one occasion he becomes deeply involved in an experiment to use molasses to bind coal dust into briquettes. The attempt fails. Coal dust everywhere in the Mead home; smoke all over. The Meads give up molasses.

The Professor's successes and failures are a great example in practical learning for young Margaret, for she is absorbing the untaught lessons of melding abstraction with reality through "his knowledge both of the concrete sequences of activities necessary to carry out any process and of the men involved—the workmen, for example, who alternately cursed and made the sign of the cross over the recalcitrant machinery." And: "Father's vivid accounts of how a street railway in

Massachusetts had failed and of the fate of a pretzel factory also gave me a sense of the way theory and practice must be related." Her father's insistence on getting the facts is also an important lesson: "You either had the facts or you did not, and the facts—not any abstract theory—dictated the conclusions."

But this man, who is so skilled in the theory and practices of the business world, is almost helpless with his own children. Mead complains that her father had virtually no body skills—he could not put his children's shoes on them without occasionally mixing left and right feet, nor brush their hair without bearing down too vigorously. However, he is a loving father, perhaps too loving, for in his concern he fears for the children's physical safety, endlessly warning them against taking chances while playing, forbidding them to climb trees or to risk danger.

But he has many appealing characteristics. One is his ability to listen to his children, to concentrate on their problems and to give them a fair hearing and sensible criticism. From the time Margaret is a small child, he teaches her how to speak in public, giving her the confidence and the techniques to reach out to an audience. She will become a skilled, relaxed speaker, at home, in a university class, at a council in a remote village, in an auditorium before thousands.

Because the Meads are educators, they are always dissatisfied with the schools available for their own children. They adopt a casual attitude about attendance in schools and classes, following a method which allows their children to learn much more than what they would get from formal classes. Some years the Mead children stay at home, others they attend local schools, depending on where they happen to live.

"From the time I was six," Mead has remarked, "the question was not when does school open, but what, if anything, is to be done about school." So, between the ages of five and seventeen, Margaret spends two years in kindergarten, one year on a half-day basis in fourth grade, and six years in high schools, having been forced to repeat some courses because of her family's moves. Elizabeth and Priscilla do not go to any kind of school until 1918, when they enter the Homquist School at New Hope, Pennsylvania, a very special private institution.

She remarks casually that in a family of educators, her parents' views about schooling were "paradoxical." Some of the moves are made to obtain a certain type of educational experience—but not necessarily in a school. The Meads disapprove of any kind of school that keeps children chained to their desks for long hours indoors. So, in place of classroom work, Emily Mead sends her children to special teachers, to learn skills they otherwise would never have. Consequently over the years young Margaret is taught drawing, painting, modelling, basketry and music; she learns how to construct a small loom, and takes woodworking lessons from a local carpenter. She believes later that this kind of education, seemingly so haphazard, actually gave her the model for the ways in which she was to organize work as an adult, with assistants, researchers or the informants in a native village, making the most of each person's talents and fitting each into an effective, productive team.

One of Margaret's most important lessons, as often, comes from Grandma Mead, who sets her to work taking notes on the behavior of her sisters and brother. Grandma Mead points out that each sister is different in temperament and has different interests. Notebooks about the children are a tradition begun by Emily Mead, who filled thirteen about Margaret, four about Richard, one about Elizabeth and none about Priscilla, for she had lost interest in this simple anthropological study. It is a task Margaret takes to "with love," for she sees the babies as "her" children (much as an anthropologist has "his" or "her" own tribe of people to study) whom she can watch, teach and raise.

Emily Mead runs into difficulties in handling this large family and her tall, somewhat erratic husband; perhaps the moves have affected her more than she expected. Whatever it is, after the birth of Priscilla in 1911, Emily Mead falls into a deep depression, and must go away for a few months, to be cared for by a medical friend of the family.

The Meads, motherless, live in a rented house in Swarthmore, near Philadelphia; the house is so cold in the winter that water freezes in the bedrooms at night. Margaret, only ten, assumes care of the children, especially the two girls, and takes her notes about Elizabeth and Priscilla, writing down how one mimics the servants, or another defies authority, commenting on the differences between Elizabeth (enthusiastic, loving and devoted) and Priscilla (self-centered but unrelentingly honest about herself). "I was fascinated by the contrasts between my sisters," she remarks.

As she grows up, she attempts to formulate the differences between each of the three girls in the family and the one boy. The differences between the girls, she decides, could not be attributed to sex. She tackles the problem more formally years afterward in one of her most famous books, *Sex and Temperament*, when she concludes that the differences between sexes and persons of each sex come from subtle interactions of heredity and environment.

Despite her parents' wide range of interests and their intellectual curiosity, they think that only a small amount of reading is good for a growing child; too much harms the eyes, and they try to limit the amount of reading engaged in by their children. For Margaret, who is an inveterate reader, books become a secret pleasure, almost a vice, indulged in at night when she is believed to be asleep, or during the day when the Meads think she is in the woods searching for botanical specimens. Aside from the rules against too many books, the children are usually allowed to do quite what they want, with broad parental direction but not too much close supervision and guidance in their odd byways.

This freedom and the intellectual curiosity that develops from it encourages young Margaret, though only eleven, to seek out some kind of religious way—"anchorage" she calls it later. Grandma Mead was once a devout Methodist; Professor Mead followed no church; Emily Mead had for a while been a Unitarian but gave up religion, apparently out of a lack of intellectual challenge. When Margaret had shown some religious yearnings at the age of seven, Emily Mead gave her the story of the Nativity of Christ in German, hoping that the events of the Incarnation would seem "crude." "All it did," remarks Mead, "was to make me regard credibility as irrelevant." She hopes for some form of religion that gives expression to an already existing faith. Church services with various immigrant maids fail to satisfy her. Somewhere there is a place for this questing child.

The Quaker Meetings at Swarthmore are a likely anchorage. But the price is enduring her father's anti-Quaker jokes. Another attempt at the Quakers, this time at the Buckingham Meeting, near Holicong, Pennsylvania, where the Meads now have a 107-acre farm. But the Meeting fails of itself: It seems to be composed of a few wealthy old people sitting in silence.

Then comes the final anchorage, one she will hold to her entire life. The rector of the Episcopal church, an Englishman named Mr. Bell, and his daughter Miss Lucia come to call on the Meads. Margaret attends a service at the church. "Almost at once I felt that the rituals of the Episcopal church were the form of religious expression for which I had been

A childhood watercolor by Margaret Mead's younger sister, Elizabeth, shows Grandma Martha Mead with Elizabeth (left) and Priscilla (right) at the gate to the family farm in Holicong, New Jersey. Elizabeth became a teacher and part-time artist; she married the noted cartoonist William Steig.

seeking," she is to state. "I had not been looking for something to believe in, for it seemed to me that a relationship to God should be based not on what you believed, but rather on what you felt."

The little church gives her not only a religious anchorage but a physical home, for she begins to haunt the rectory. She develops a deep friendship for Miss Lucia, "the most humanly sensitive person I had ever known." She takes on the problems of the church as her own. The other children in the congregation attend services only because they are told to by their parents, but Margaret is a willing member of the parish because she has made a free choice. "I enjoyed prayer. I enjoyed church. I worried over the small size of our congregation."

She begins to explore the world a little. One of her favorite trips is to New York; she stays in Brooklyn with her young godmother, Isabel Ely Lord, who had been her sponsor at baptism. Isabel teaches art at Pratt Institute. Margaret crosses to Manhattan by the DeKalb Avenue streetcar whenever she can. She falls in love with the city.

During this period—she is approaching her teens—Margaret is sent on a regular basis to the tiny Buckingham Friends School, an institution so small and hampered by the lack of funds that it has only one teacher for three grades, the eighth and the first two of high school. The school is so desperately poor that Margaret finds herself studying Latin from the same grammar texts that her grandmother has used two generations earlier.

After Buckingham comes one year in a public high school. When the family moves to Doylestown and Margaret transfers to a new school, she is forced to undergo a number of subjects she had already taken. She complains that she had to read Cicero for the second time, John Milton's *L'Allegro* and *Il Penseroso* for the third. But at Doylestown, no one has to study hard, and the students take time off whenever it pleases them.

Margaret is a child who likes challenges, who meets problems head on. A large amount of creativity is demanded, otherwise she will fall into the undemanding patterns of her classmates. She writes reviews for the local newspaper, helps launch a school magazine, puts on an amateur theatrical with friends; she begins to write seriously. Poetry, short plays, a diary demand her time.

"In school I always felt that I was special and different, set apart in a way that could not be attributed to any gift I had, but only to my background—to the education given me by my grandmother and to the explicit academic interests of my parents. . . . But at the same time I searched for a greater intensity than the world around me offered."

What career is she to pursue? A career is expected, for she is not going to drift into the regulated, restrictive life of a woman in a small Pennsylvania or New Jersey town. Alert, intelligent, talented, outspoken, Margaret cannot let herself moulder. A whole world is waiting for her to explore. With her mother and grandmother as role models, she expects to be both a professional woman and a wife and mother. She speculates about being a lawyer, a writer, a minister's wife with six children, even a nun.

The spring of 1917 has arrived. It is the year in which the United States enters World War I on the side of Britain and France against Germany and Austria-Hungary, a war that has been raging with frightful casualties since 1914. At a school prom Mead meets a young man named Luther Cressman, the young brother of one of her teachers at Doylestown. Margaret and Luther spend the night dancing. Luther is four years older than Margaret, a senior at Penn State. He is thinking of entering the ministry, his mother's idea. According to Mead's friends he is a good athlete, drives a car (automobiles were then not so common as they are now), and takes beautiful photographs. She thinks that Luther Cressman, with his slim build and engaging smile and wry sense of humor (but he can be serious, too), is handsome. The old snapshots show him as a typical young man of the period, fitting the pattern of male looks of his time, with a stiff high collar, neatly parted, brushed hair, a tie knotted tightly: It is the type of male look exemplified by the Arrow shirt ads of the age, a type so standardized that "Arrow shirt" became a term for conventional. Straight Arrow.

Margaret and Luther, in love (or is it mere infatuation?— from the distance one cannot tell her true feelings), do not see each other again until Christmas, when suddenly they become secretly engaged. Luther's plans to enter the ministry are now set and Mead looks forward to being a clergyman's wife in a big, old rectory with lots of children. First Luther must go fight the enemy: He has to attend officer's training camp.

Margaret takes over the job of running the Mead farm in Holicong; she cooks for the family and the hired hands, and works at the local Red Cross. Though she writes Luther a four-page letter every day, she still has not told her parents of the engagement.

The months move swiftly: The war ends on November 11, 1918. The Meads give up the Holicong farm and move to New Hope, a few miles away. Luther is demobilized and at last Margaret thinks it time to inform her parents of the coming marriage, a marriage that will take place not sooner but later, for she has not yet completed her education.

Ambiguities surround the couple, at least from Margaret's side. They will not marry for five years, until she finishes college and has done some postgraduate work. In all this time she seems to have loved Luther, yet there is a strange air of a lack of commitment, for sixty years later she can write:

> Father offered me a trip around the world and a very liberal allowance if I would give up my plan to get married. He was moved to do this by my grandmother's conviction that I was getting married because, in my mind, this was the expected thing for a girl to do after college. . . . In addition, he did not like my choice of a husband.

The crucial sentence I have reserved for special attention (it goes in the place of the ellipses above). Mead writes, "She [my grandmother] was right in this judgment." That is, this very unconventional young woman was, in the long run, being quite conventional, at least for the time. One senses a great lack of passion in young Margaret for her fiancé: She had more interest in the Samoans.

The Importance of Being a Woman

AND NOW COMES MEAD'S first great test of being a woman: She wants to go to college. She has her eye on Wellesley, for which she had been preparing by taking three years of French, for languages were one of that college's requirements. A crisis is precipitated: Her father opposes Margaret's going to college. The reason for his opposition is simple: "In the spring [of 1918] my father suffered a lot of losses in one of his private business ventures." Yet Mead is determined that she will go to Wellesley.

Tension mounts rapidly on both sides. But rather than face the issue squarely—we are getting her version—or perhaps as the result of his inability to convince his daughter that he has no money ("I had always been a match for Father," she has remarked), Professor Mead asks a doctor friend to try to dissuade Margaret.

The physician misjudges his audience. He offers a rambling and irrelevant argument: Margaret's hands are too small, she never has done a day's work in her life, she'll make a poor wife, she'd better study nursing. "Hearing this," she says, still vibrating with anger over the incident, "I exploded in one of the few fits of feminist rage I have ever had."

Somewhat chastened by the report he has received from

his friend, Professor Mead allows his wife to persuade him to
let Margaret have her way. Somehow the money for tuition
and expenses is available. But Margaret will not go to Wellesley. Emily Mead suggests that Margaret attend DePauw, her
father's own alma mater, a well-known institution of moder-
ate size located in Greencastle, Indiana. It is a kind of compromise: Her father has "won" by not sending his daughter
to Wellesley; Margaret has really won by getting him to pay
for college after all, despite "his financial uncertainties and
worries."

Mead again has contradictory attitudes: In *Blackberry Winter* she can say both that "I greatly respected the way my
father thought" and that "I was prepared to combat to the
finish his conservative, money-bound judgments" and still
preface this statement by admitting "his right to spend his
money as he wished." DePauw is far away. Margaret knows
only Philadelphia, south Jersey, a few towns in eastern Pennsylvania and New York, which she has visited often. In prepa-
ration for the coming year Margaret designs some dresses to
wear at DePauw. They are run up by the family dressmaker.
She has never been noted for style in clothing—she favors the
shapeless—and her first designs are, to say the least, unusual.
One is "an evening dress that was to represent a field of
wheat with poppies against a blue sky with white clouds."
Romantic but dreadful is her later verdict. But she soon has
a wardrobe of clothing, which does not resemble anything
the girls at DePauw, a rather snobbish, style-conscious mid-
western college, actually wear.

Now seventeen, Margaret leaves the warmth of the family
home for college, taking with her pictures of the Bengali
nationalist poet Rabindranath Tagore and the Russian revolu-
tionary Catherine Bushovka, the latter a special favorite of
her mother, and letters to women in various sororities. De-
Pauw is a place "to which students had come for fraternity

Margaret Mead, nineteen, spends a not very happy year at DePauw before transferring to Barnard in New York City to complete her education.

life, for football games, and for establishing the kind of rap-
port with other people that would make them good Rotarians
in later life and their wives good members of the garden
club."

For a moment DePauw seems friendly; Mead meets girls
with whom she had corresponded over the summer, but
quickly the awakening comes. The college is a far step from
the idealistic, egalitarian principles of the Mead family, and
she meets a snobbism she had not experienced previously. In
her own home "no one suggested that we had any superiors,
only people who had more money or were more interested
in validating their special position." But in DePauw she is
"confronted by the snobbery and cruelty of the sorority system at its worst." The social groups at the college are stra-
tified and rigidly organized, and to her irrational. When she
wears her unusual homemade dresses one of her previously
friendly correspondents turns away, never to speak to her
again.

She finds herself part of a minority, ostracized by the sororities, for along with her strange clothing, she has an eastern
accent and is one of five people in the freshman class who do
not belong to an evangelical church. As an Episcopalian, she
cannot even belong to the local YWCA. Among the outcasts
there are a Roman Catholic, a Greek Orthodox, a Lutheran
and a Jew. To further compound her difficulties in this coedu-
cational college, she realizes on the basis of one of her classes,
which has two girls and a dozen boys, that when the girls get
better marks than the boys, they suffer for their excellence.
On the one hand, she does not want to do bad work in order
to receive the approbation of the young men; on the other,
neither does she want to overshadow them to the point
where they dislike her.

The year at DePauw is her first and only experience with
any kind of discrimination, though only a mild one, and, she

speculates, it is virtually nothing compared to what people in actual minorities undergo.

> It is very difficult to know how to evaluate how essential it is to have one's soul seared by the great injustices of one's own time—being born a serf or slave, a woman believed to have no mind or no soul, a black man or woman in a white man's world, a Jew among Christians who make a virtue of anti-Semitism, a miner among those who thought it good sport to hire Pinkertons to shoot down miners on strike. Such experiences sear the soul. They make their victims ache with bitterness and rage, with compassion for fellow sufferers or with blind determination to escape even on the backs of fellow sufferers. . . . Injustice experienced in the flesh, in deeply wounded flesh, is the stuff out of which change explodes.

Mead feels like an exile. Because she does not belong to a sorority she has no dates. She makes one friend, a girl named Katherine Rothenberger, whom Mead gets elected to a class office by exploiting sorority rivalries. Unhappy at DePauw, she decides there is no choice but to transfer to an all-woman college. Another small-town college does not attract her, for she believes that such an atmosphere stifles the mind. It is New York that has the great call, so she persuades her father to let her transfer to Barnard College, part of Columbia University, in uptown Manhattan. New York has another attraction: Luther Cressman is there, and in the excitement of the big city she feels that she can have "a life that demonstrated in a more real and dramatic form that I was not among the rejected and unchosen."

Barnard brings her "the kind of student life that matched my earlier dreams," for here Mead is no longer an outsider but finds congenial friends, challenging courses and a stimulating intellectual environment. And Luther, studying at the General Theological Seminary, is not far away.

She immediately becomes friends with a group of intelligent, progressive, outspoken young women whose wide range of interests coincides with hers. American life is changing rapidly in the postwar period. American youth especially is asserting itself through rebellion, experimentation, questionings of elders, challenges to authority and institutions. She and her friends think of themselves as outcasts and radicals. (It is, of course, a romantic notion.) A sense of alienation is a key mood. But it is not the kind of alienation that she experienced in her year at DePauw, one of not fitting into a milieu because of clothing or accent or interests. This is far more widespread, for the women are aware of social problems, of sex in its various forms, of psychoanalysis and other new disciplines, and of radical politics.

As a means of challenging and confusing their elders, they take an amusing form of self-denigration: Each year Mead and her friends adopt a derogatory name for themselves. One year the group calls itself "a mental and moral muss," a term used by the head of one of the Barnard dormitories in frustration at being unable to control the lives of the students. The group thinks the term is apt. The second year, because of its liberal and radical attitudes, it is "Communist Morons," and the third, in a phrase it prefers to others, "Ash Can Cats," a name given it by one of its most popular teachers, Minor Latham, who was probably referring to a New York group of realist painters, the Ash Can School, who worked with vivid, contemporary material—life as it is lived in the great city. These nicknames are an innocuous kind of protest proudly borne, but puzzling to older generations more accustomed to quiet behavior on the part of young women.

They write poetry of fair competence. One of the group,

Léonie Adams, is to become a major American poet. They join picket lines, help with mailings for the clothing workers' union, invite liberal speakers to an organization known as the Sunday Night Club (Mead is the president). It is the time of the trial of Sacco and Vanzetti, two Italian-American anarchists accused of murder during a holdup. The case has become a symbol of the struggle between radicals and conservatives. The group holds a fund-raising meeting for the two men but can raise only $25.

The Broadway theater, in a creative, expansive, vibrant period, also gets their attention. One of the big hits of the time is *Rain*, a play based on a short story by the English writer Somerset Maugham. Jeanne Eagels is the star and the play runs a long time. The setting is Samoa; the story is about a tragic conflict between a reforming, harsh missionary and a prostitute trying to escape to a safer world.

When Calvin Coolidge (then vice president of the United States) asks rhetorically in a magazine article, "Are the 'Reds' Stalking Our College Women?" Léonie Adams replies in *The Barnard Bulletin*, "Cheer Up, Mr. Coolidge," for she thinks young American women have more political maturity than the vice president gives them credit for. "We belonged to a generation of young women who felt extraordinarily free," Mead says later. Though they are not conscious of it at the time, they are among the forerunners of the present women's movement. "We learned loyalty to women." The group believes that no woman need subordinate her friendship with other women in favor of men. They feel liberated from the ties and bonds that hampered their mothers and grandmothers. "[We were] free from the demand to marry unless we chose to do so, free to postpone marriage while we did other things, free from the need to bargain and hedge that had restricted women of earlier generations. . . . We did not bargain with men." They are forming their own identities, as people, not subject to the prevailing attitudes that put women in secondary roles.

In her teens Mead had wanted to be a creative writer. She wrote numerous poems and prose pieces, along with reviews for the local newspaper. In her year at DePauw she continued to write. In her first year at Barnard she expects that she will write professionally. But at last she accepts the fact that creative writing is not her true interest. "I did not have the superlative talent . . . that was crucial for success in the contemporary world," she admits.

She considers politics, too, but rejects it as a career, because political success is too short-term and too demanding. Then, in her junior year, she becomes interested in psychology and begins to explore it. There are many new developments in the field, a number of them due to the work of the Viennese psychiatrist Sigmund Freud, then in his mid-sixties. Freud had pioneered in probing various aspects of the subconscious mind; his work already at that time has had a profound effect upon the entire world, being applied to numerous other scientific and cultural disciplines, from medicine to anthropology to art and literature. There is scarcely a field which in some way or another does not react to the implications of Freud's thinking about sex, the family, the role of the individual and each person's subconscious.

By her senior year Mead is fully committed to psychology as a career. But two courses she takes this last year at Barnard are to change her life irrevocably. One is a course in the psychological aspects of culture given by William Fielding Ogburn, a follower of Freud's theories; the other is a course in anthropology given by Franz Boas, who is developing new approaches in his own discipline.

Boas, a small, slight man, born in 1858, obtained his Ph.D. in physics in Germany with a dissertation on the color of sea water. He soon switched from physics to anthropology, a field which until late in the nineteenth century had been an unorganized and undisciplined science.

Much early anthropology was the work of Westerners in foreign lands who had gone abroad for other reasons. Many of them were originally missionaries or in the military, or were colonial administrators or businessmen who seized the unparalleled opportunities to study the strange societies among which they worked or travelled.

One of the most famous early anthropologists was the brilliant Englishman Sir Richard Francis Burton, who had gone to India as an eighteen-year-old officer serving under the East India Company and who went on to become a famous linguist and the explorer of exotic and primitive societies in India, Africa and the Middle East. His works such as *Sindh, the Unhappy Valley* and his three-volume account of his trip to Mecca (disguised as a Muslim from Afghanistan) contain material that can never be duplicated today. Burton was the founder of the organization which later became the Anthropological Institute of Great Britain. Still, he was an adventurer, and though an unsurpassed observer (and participant) he was not a theorist.

Another typical example of the nineteenth-century anthropologist was the British missionary H.R. Coddington, who lived in the South Pacific, then a very wild and primitive area, from 1863 to 1887 and was able to record island ways before they were destroyed by white encroachment; his *The Melanesians*, originally published in 1891, is still available and remains a classic work. Such men, by the dozens, if not the hundreds, laid the foundation for modern anthropology.

Though men like Burton and Coddington and their fellows, men of unusual courage, wit and sensitivity as well as curiosity, were able to record unusual and exotic cultures in detail and with insight, they gave little thought to theory. However,

nineteenth-century anthropology did gain some form from
the views of two men: the Englishman Edward Burnett Tylor
(1832–1917), and the American Lewis Henry Morgan (1818–
1881), both of whom were able to see a general shape to the
development of mankind.

Tylor is usually considered to be the first professional anthropologist, being the first person to teach it formally at a
university. Tylor disagreed with the view of previous
European writers (mainly French and English) that the
American Indians were examples of degenerated descendants of civilized man. In *Primitive Culture*, published in
1871, Tylor stated that culture evolved from the simple to
the complex, and that all societies passed through three
basic stages of development: savagery, barbarism, and civilization.

Morgan, an upstate New York lawyer, represented the Iro-
quois Indians in a land grant dispute and was adopted by the
tribe, thus gaining an unparalleled opportunity to study their
lives and culture. He gave up law to devote his time fully to
anthropology. In his best known work, *Ancient Society*
(1877), he developed Tylor's theory of the three stages into
a more complex structure, saying that the development of
mankind came from a "few primary germs of thought." He
believed that the family evolved through six different stages,
beginning with a "horde living in promiscuity" and passing
on to a stage where groups of brothers married groups
of sisters, to the highest stage, that of monogamy, with a
self-contained family unit possessing private, not communal
property. Later anthropologists could find no historical or
contemporary examples of Morgan's six stages, though the
German socialist Karl Marx was impressed by his analysis of
the development of the family and carried it a step further
to the stage where the monogamous family, private property

and the state would someday cease to exist and a form of "communism" analogous to Morgan's view of primitive society would develop.

When Boas appears to contest Morgan's assumptions and conceptions, it is a time when anthropology needs a second wind and some new insights and challenges to its hardening theories. Boas believes that the entire field must be reexamined. He has no use for any single theory of the origins, forms or development of the world's cultures, neither those proposed by Tylor and Morgan nor others that might posit that mankind came from a single source or a small number of archaic originating societies. Boas accuses his predecessors in the profession of working from inadequate data. Worse, many had not even gone into the field, basing their conclusions on the diaries, reports and travel books of merchants, missionaries and explorers, who, not being scientists, recorded only fragments of cultures, usually the odd and intriguing aspects. No wonder primitive people seem so "foreign."

Boas stresses the enormous importance of cultural variation, and he emphasizes the need to work in the field to collect vast amounts of material to be employed as the basis for interpretation and theory. An echo of Professor Mead's insistence on getting the facts before proposing theories is seen here. Boas's radical approach to anthropology, in which nothing is to be assumed and all is to be studied in each culture, sets a high standard for Mead to follow in her own work.

Boas is a challenging, engaging lecturer, formal, "somewhat frightening." His lectures are polished and clear, but he has the annoying habit of paying attention only to students who need help. Mead is ignored, but instead of taking it as a compliment, she has an understandable feeling of insecurity.

Perhaps she is too bad a student for Boas to aid, she worries. But at the end of the term he compliments her on her valuable contributions to classroom discussions.

In her own home Mead had grown up with many of the implied tenets of anthropology. "I was accustomed to regard all the races of man as equal and to look at all human cultures as comparable." By the spring of her final year at Barnard she seriously considers anthropology as a career, even though she is working on her paper for her master's degree in psychology. The subject, which is a suggestion of Boas's, for he has done some work on Italian-Americans, is a continuation of Emily Mead's work with the Hammonton immigrants.

Mead's thesis is entitled "Intelligence Tests of Italian and American Children." Boas had postulated that a new environment would produce changes in the immigrants' children. Measurements made by Emily Mead showed that the form of the children's heads had changed, confirming Boas's own work. It was, she said, an innovative study of the effect of environment on characteristics that previously had been considered unchangeable. Thus the work of the two Mead women supports Boas's supposition.

Boas's assistant is a woman named Ruth Benedict, who had entered anthropology three years earlier. She is a quiet, highly intelligent person, fifteen years older than Mead, and difficult to know. But young Margaret has a great liking for Benedict and relies on her judgment and opinions. They help each other with work, take on each other's responsibilities and share worries about their chosen discipline. "I began to know her not only as a teacher but also as a friend," she says of Benedict. "I continued to call her 'Mrs. Benedict' until I got my degree and then, almost imperceptibly, our relationship became one of colleagues and close friends."

Benedict is a slim, unpretentious woman, a great beauty who often feels ugly, wearing the same dress, hat and coat days, even weeks, on end. She has had a difficult marriage to a famous natural scientist, Stanley Benedict (her maiden name was Fulton), and after several attempts at finding some meaning to her life, including teaching and running day-care centers, settled on anthropology, entering the Columbia Graduate School in 1921 to study under Boas. In the future she will write two major works, *Patterns of Culture* (1934) and *The Chrysanthemum and the Sword: Patterns of Japanese Culture* (1946), plus an important, controversial pamphlet (with Gene Weltfish), *The Races of Mankind* (1942). Her first major field trip comes in the summer of 1924, when she visits the Zuñi; the next year she studies them again, along with their neighbors, the Cochiti. Living under primitive conditions, she writes home that her diet with the Cochiti consists of rice and raisins, enlivened by three cans of tomato soup found in the trading post—a statement made more in amazement than complaint.

Benedict, Mead remarks, humanized Boas's formal lectures, putting his general principles into specific terms and examples. Benedict, whose brilliance brought much jealousy from colleagues, thought that culture could be viewed as "personality writ large," each historical culture representing a many-generational process of paring, sifting, adapting and elaborating upon the life-style of a people. Each culture in turn shapes the ways of living, the choices and personality of the people born and living within it. "I feel about it [anthropological work] just as I do about a novelist's getting down his character with the correct motivations, etc. . . . What I'm fundamentally interested in is the character of the culture and the relation of that institutionalized character to the individual of that culture"—that is the underlying theme of Benedict's approach. She has a profound influence on Mead. Anthropology is what Mead now wants, but she is being wooed in other directions.

The problem is a frustrating one. A lunch with Benedict brings an amazing turn. Mead, a more voluble conversationalist than Benedict, is worrying aloud over her future: Should she continue with psychology, or go deeper into sociology? They are parallel, sometimes interrelated and interdependent fields, but one must adhere to one or the other. Benedict remarks in her shy, off-hand manner, "Professor Boas and I have nothing to offer but an opportunity to do work that matters." An unexpected solution! For Mead, anthropology is to be the direction of her life.

It is the spring of 1923. She graduates from Barnard with her B.A., with plans to go into graduate school under Boas and Benedict. Ogburn has offered her a job as an assistant in his department of economics and sociology. In the fall she marries Luther Cressman, an event that draws nationwide attention in small news boxes, for this modern young woman emerges from the ceremony in the tiny Episcopalian church in Buckingham, Pennsylvania, still Miss Mead. She refuses to become Mrs. Cressman, even with the marriage vows. "What is the world coming to?" is the observation of a number of people. The decision is not one of principle but of preference, says Mead, but the statement is on the ambiguous side, for she then adds that she is following her mother's belief that women should maintain their identities in all instances in preference to being submerged.

But all goes well, at least for the immediate present. Miss Mead and Mr. Cressman, now an ordained minister, find a small apartment in Manhattan. It is like many young couple's first apartment: two tiny rooms, a small vestibule, a two-burner stove atop the half-size refrigerator, secondhand

Luther Cressman, Margaret Mead's first husband, here seen at the General Theological Seminary in New York City. He was ordained a minister but soon shifted his vocation to that of anthropologist; later he became an archeologist, specializing in American Indian sites.

furniture, bookcases built as the result of Mead's childhood training in carpentry, hamburgers in various guises, numerous dinner parties for four, the most the apartment can accommodate. Luther has a graduate fellowship and is also an assistant pastor of a small church in an outlying Brooklyn community known as East New York. The church is an exhausting subway ride away, and Mead rarely makes the trip to see her husband in his pastoral role.

In the first bloom of their engagement, she had looked forward to the fulfillment of her childhood dream of being the wife of a minister and the mother of six in a drafty old rectory. But Luther's vocation is weakening, slipping away. He is considering abandoning the ministry, to take up sociology. The first year of the marriage, she will recall, is a time of "eminent peace." But is it too peaceful? There are none of the arguments and quarrels that test a marriage, that lead two people to come to a deeper understanding and knowledge of each other. Mead enjoys the absence of stress, for she carries memories of tensions between her parents, of her father's infidelities and her mother's rigidities.

This peace, however, seems to be on the surface. An undercurrent of unrest lies deeper, she can note on later reflection, and gives her poetry of the time as an indication. Analyzing her work afterward, she sees secret fears and worries. In one poem she compares herself to mercury but does not pursue the image: but—"My soul you cannot shatter/Ne'er hold in your hand." She is still an independent woman. In another poem she feels throttled by weeds. She wonders if she has not accepted marriage as an easy way in preference to a more adventurous, dangerous path, and in another poem speaks of tortured precious flesh but "You could not ease the pain."

One receives the impression that Mead had drifted into marriage because it was there. Has her relationship with Luther involved deep emotions? Probably not, for "peace" not "love" is the description she gives of the marriage. No problems to overcome, no pitting of one strength against another, of one personality against an equally strong-willed one. Blandness. So it seems a matter of course that by the fall of 1924 she and Cressman are agreed to go in separate directions for a year, to follow their individual interests.

So far as her marriage to Luther is concerned, this is the end, at least psychologically. Their marriage has been, as she is likely to remark from time to time in explanation of what happened, "a student marriage," one which she finally entered because it was the expected thing to do. The marriage has faded away rather rapidly, and seemingly without qualm or deep emotion. But still they will continue on what seems to be a superficial basis for almost another year.

Summer, 1924: The British Association for the Advancement of Science meets in Toronto. It is what is now called an "interdisciplinary" conference. As there are only a handful of anthropologists in the entire world, an even smaller handful can attend the Toronto talks. It is an exciting time: Jung's recently published theory of psychological types is argued over. Work among the Northwest Coast Bella Bella, work in the Arctic, work here and there, is presented. Mead feels a bit left out. Everyone has a special field. "My" people. "My Bella Bella." "My Eskimos." "My Italians at Hammonton" is not an impressive phrase. She, too, wants her own people, exotic people.

She must go into the field. But which field? She discusses the problem with Boas. Interesting new studies can be made in the way in which new customs in a new country, such as the United States, or new ways of life in an old country are related to older ones. It is the theme that guided her research in adaptation among the children in Hammonton.

Boas, however, has other ideas. He believes that sufficient work has already been done on the problems of cultural influence and borrowing. The questions he introduces are intriguing ones: Are the problems of adolescence shared by all cultures, or are they unique in certain ones? What in adolescence stems from the conditioning of a particular culture? What is inherent in the adolescent stage of psychobiological development with its various periods of growth, impulse and random discrepancies? He wants Mead to study the adolescent girl in a primitive society.

Now a struggle begins between the shrewd, experienced, elderly Boas and the shrewd, inexperienced, young Mead. Boas wants her to pursue this particular subject, but it must be pursued in a "safe" area. Mead, who is willing to compromise on the subject, wants to select her own area in which to work. That area is Polynesia, which was the subject of both a seminar report she had prepared and her doctoral dissertation. She is specifically interested in the Tuamotu Islands, a very remote group in French Polynesia, where life is primitive and the native culture is being rapidly destroyed by contact with the whites.

No, says Boas, with all the authority of his position and years. He is concerned that she would be too isolated in the Tuamotus, which are but infrequently served by ship. But where is he to send his most promising student?

There is no time to lose, for all over the globe "primitive," unaffected peoples—that is, those virtually untouched by the Western world—are disappearing. Languages and techniques of living, of hunting, fishing, farming, of arts, crafts and music, of government, marriage and death customs are rapidly vanishing. In the 1920's there is only a small number of anthropologists to carry on the vast work of studying disappearing and dying cultures, and few successors to count on: There are only four graduate students at Columbia and not many more at all the other universities. Boas could survey a map of the world with a sinking heart and see his smattering

of troops facing insurmountable challenges. Siberia, sections
of the Low Countries of Europe and parts of the Pacific will
soon be lost to modernization. He can send Mead to any of
these. But—for Siberia she needs Russian and Chinese, for the
Low Countries French, Dutch, German and even medieval
Latin, and for the Pacific "only" French and German. But the
Pacific is dangerous, and Boas fears that Mead, so small and
frail looking (she is five feet two and a half, and weighs ninety-
eight pounds), will succumb to some illness or other. He suggests instead the American Indian, possibly the most studied
subject of any in anthropology. But more work can still be
done. His suggestion seems more like an order. Mead refuses.

The battle intensifies. She will not do fieldwork among the
American Indians. She is determined on Polynesia. Too many
people are already at work on the Indians, too little is being
done in the Pacific. Boas is adamant. Impasse.

The struggle takes an interesting turn. Boas has power.
Mead realizes she needs to change the battleground, to force
Boas to fight on a different level. She approaches her father,
not as her ally but as a rival to Boas. She tells him that Boas
is attempting to force her to enter a field of study which has
no interest for her. She wants to go to Polynesia, not an Indian
reservation.

Professor Mead, in order to rescue his daughter from Boas's
domination, offers her a trip around the world. She can work
in Polynesia and then continue her voyage.

Victory for the young woman, but, she is to write later, the
situation still bothers her, that her father has thus sacrificed
his own long-planned trip to Europe. It is, she admits bluntly,
an act of manipulation, pitting two men against each other in
order to attain her own purposes. Whether or not there were
alternate methods of breaking the impasse she did not consider at the time, nor consider half a century later.

In retrospect the "ethics of manipulation" concern her.
The two older men have been used; as a young woman she
seems not to have given much thought to what she did; but
in her seventies she tries to come to terms with the situation:
"When I seriously turned my attention to the whole question
of manipulation, I began to understand that one should not
use either a person's strength or his weaknesses against him."
How is one to handle such a situation? "The only course that
is ethically justified is an appeal to strength—not in order to
throw one's opponent by means of his own strength, but on
the grounds that reliance on strength will work for the good."
People, she states, will operate not in the worst manner but
constructively and honestly.

In the end Boas surrenders. His best student is going to
Polynesia whether he agrees or not. But some minor compromises are now in order. In place of the remote Tuamotu
Islands Margaret will select an area where there is a regular
boat service of at least one boat every three weeks. Her
choice is Samoa, where there is a United States naval base and
a steamer from Honolulu on the stipulated three-week basis.

Samoa is still a fertile area for study, though it is hardly an
unknown land. Foreign powers, missionaries, vagabonds,
traders, writers, ethnologists and anthropologists have already been there. Much is known about the native people,
though no one has yet found out what a Samoan girl experiences in growing up.

Robert Louis Stevenson had written many articles from the
South Pacific, some about Samoa; he had spent his last years
on the island of Upolu, across the strait from Pago Pago,
where Mead will begin her work. *Rain* helped make the
name of Samoa known, though the public had been more
interested in the collapse of a missionary's moral code than
Samoan life. At least the name Samoa is almost as well known
as Honolulu or even Tahiti, where the bedeviled French

painter Paul Gauguin had passed his last drunken, diseased years. So Mead prepares for Samoa.

Boas, now that the crisis is past, does his best for Mead. He obtains a grant for her from the National Research Council. He admits, "I myself am not pleased with this idea of her going to the tropics for a long stay," but obviously Samoa is better than the Tuamotus. He tells Benedict that he knows "Margaret is high-strung and emotional," but to prevent her from going now would create more problems than those posed by the trip.

She packs. She gets her shots. By today's standards of anthropological equipment what she takes is laughable, less even than what a well-prepared tourist would carry in jetting off for a world tour. She has a small strongbox for money and papers, a small folding Kodak, a portable typewriter, six large fat notebooks, typing paper and carbon sheets. She is warned not to take silk dresses, since silk "rots in the tropics." (In Samoa she finds that the American navy wives dress in silk.) She has no lamp. "When field workers were poor," she remarks of the past, the tendency was "to take along as little as possible and to make very few plans."

Margaret and Luther have a brief vacation together and then set off on their separate ways, the wife to Samoa, the husband to Europe. She is to meet Luther again, in Europe, but more as friends—one might say even as casual friends—than as spouses, keeping up for a short while the outward appearance of marriage.

The Quadrangle

SIX MONTHS AT THE NAVY medical post at Tau, on Samoa's remote Manu'a group, go by as if in a tropical dream. Tau, a mere eight by eleven miles, is "the only place where I can live in a white household and still be in the midst of these villages all the time," Mead writes home. (She writes long letters, often to Grandma Mead, which are copied and recopied by her family and sent to everyone interested.) Staying with the Holts provides her with the advantages of substantial American food (Samoan food is "too starchy," she tells her family) and a good American bed, while allowing her a free run of the villages on Tau (there are four clustered together) to study and talk, dance, bathe with the teenage girls, be treated as royalty (she is twice adopted into the families of chiefs). The Samoans call her Malekita, their version of Margaret; Malekita is also the name of the last queen of Manu'a. She also receives a ceremonial name, Fuailelagi, "Flower of Heaven."

The heat bothers her. "This is not an easy climate to work in," she writes Boas. She thinks her efficiency is diminished by 50 percent from the heat, and would be even less if she could not live in the navy post and had to stay with a Samoan family. But in the same letter she can boast, "I am quite well and standing the climate with commendable fortitude."

The heat intensifies. Millions of flies. Working in the Samoan houses, talking to people, listening, ears attuned for every detail, every nuance of Samoan life, she is bothered by the climate. The open houses are not so comfortable as one might imagine. Sitting cross-legged on the pebbled floors (on which Samoans walk with bare feet) brings endless aches. Sticky heat, heavy. Her skin feels as if it will peel off in layers. Strange buzzing in her head from continued concentration on what the girls are saying. The buzz of the flies, the buzz of voices. The Samoan meals she is forced to take. The ceremonies. A pig is sacrificed to celebrate a birth: Blood splatters on her cotton dress. The heat is broken when a hurricane strikes, leveling the village. Mead and the Holts with their babies take refuge in a concrete water tank. Only five houses are left standing.

Departure time comes too soon. Now she is nostalgic. Exchanges of gifts. For the Samoans from Malekita, sheets of writing paper, needles, cigarettes, ink, pencils, matches, onions, thread. From the Samoans, mats, flowers, a chicken. At last, among the swaying palms and rolling surf, the idyllic beaches and the round thatch-roofed houses, and the ordered, hierarchical life of the Samoans she has come to love so well, Mead, her work completed, farewells said, packs up her precious notes and rolls of Kodak film for the boat trip to the main island of Tutuila. Her six months in Manu'a among the teenage girls, so lacking in the stresses and strains that mark American adolescence, are to be known as one of the most famous field trips of anthropology.

At Pago Pago she packs for the continuation of her trip around the world, for she will return home via Europe. She makes a brief excursion to Vaitogi, where she had first been instructed in Samoan etiquette and customs. Only now does she realize that she is homesick after half a year in the field.

Loneliness and the lack of affection, occupational hazards of the anthropologist, have beset her. Letters from home have been rare—some arrive in Samoa after she has left—and she never receives the reply in time from Boas and Ruth Benedict about whether or not she has been following the proper field methods. Ahead lies a rendezvous not only with Benedict but with Luther and a Barnard friend, Louise Rosenblatt.

The steamer on which she travels from Pago Pago to Australia runs into one of the worst storms of the century. Many ships are lost, but her boat survives, and finally makes port safely in Sydney, where she changes to a large steamship.

In Australia Mead finds herself again in a familiar world: Here she can attend concerts, carry on conversations in her own language—a language she can speak without worrying about the niceties of rank and etiquette—and enjoy the benefits of an advanced society. Fate, which had sent her to Samoa instead of to an American Indian reservation or the remote islands of French Polynesia, now intervenes again. A dock strike holds up the ship. Most of the passengers take hotel rooms ashore, but Mead, with no extra money, stays aboard ship. The dining room steward puts her at the same table with a young man from New Zealand, who is also forced to remain aboard.

Her table companion is a psychology student on the way to England to take up a scholarship at Cambridge University, awarded to him for an essay about dreams. His name is Reo Fortune. She says, "It was like meeting a stranger from another planet, but a stranger with whom I had a great deal in common," for New Zealand was then a provincial backwater, outside the slow lines of communication from the rest of the world. Fortune has never seen a play performed professionally, nor seen a painting by a great artist, nor heard live symphonic music. But he has been reading omnivorously whatever comes to hand.

Fortune's most recent interest is psychoanalysis. He has read Sigmund Freud, whose work on dreams as spokesmen for the subconscious has been attracting much attention, but he is especially interested in the writings of a Cambridge don named W.H.R. Rivers, whose studies in physiology, psychoanalysis and ethnology are known among professionals all over the world. Evolution, the unconscious mind and its early origins in man's precursors were subjects of Rivers' work and he was critical of Freud's theories.

Fortune's essay takes Rivers as a basic theme. He tells Mead that without changing the basic premises, Rivers had stood Freud on his head, making fear, not sexual drives, the motivating force in man. Much of Fortune's work in dreams and sleep has been done upon himself. He is curious, for example, whether all the dreams dreamt in one night are the same dream, a question which had been raised by Freud.

On the voyage Mead begins to record her own dreams for Reo: She finds that one night she has eight dreams on a major theme and two on subsidiary themes—partial confirmation of Reo's inquiries. He will publish one of her dreams in his first book, *The Mind in Sleep.*

The two young people have much to talk about. Not only are they both the same age, but both are professional scientists.

The ship moves on slowly, casually, spending days in one port after another. The weeks drag on as it steams through the sultry seas. Margaret and Reo spend all their time together. Their conversations are intense, emotional. The bond becomes more than professional. "We were falling in love, with all the possibility of a relationship I felt was profoundly unsuitable," she writes in *Blackberry Winter.* "Reo was so young, so inexperienced, so fiercely ambitious, and so possessively jealous of any fleeting glance I gave another person."

Is he rebounding from an earlier affair? He tells her he had been passionately in love with a girl named Eileen in New Zealand, but she had eventually refused him.

They pass Ceylon, the Arabian peninsula, go through the Suez Canal, see Sicily in the distance. At last the ship arrives at Marseilles, where Margaret is to meet Luther. Should she continue to England with Reo, or go ashore to meet her husband? The ship docks. She and Reo are deep in intense conversation. Finally Mead is able to pull herself together: She sees Luther standing on the dock, wondering what has happened to her.

"That is one of the moments I would take back and live differently if I could," she writes.

She goes ashore to meet Luther, leaving Reo to continue alone.

In France Luther shows her the things he has discovered during his time there. They meet her college friend, Louise Rosenblatt. Mead is constantly preoccupied with memories of Reo. They meet briefly in Paris. At last she decides in favor of Luther. A firm decision. But there is much she withholds from us in *Blackberry Winter*. Clearly she is still in touch with Reo. Luther must go home early to a new job. She remains in Europe, meeting Ruth Benedict in Rome. She is to have a rendezvous with Reo in Paris. He crosses the Channel; her train from Italy is held up. Frustration. They can meet only at the last minute, when her ship sails for New York and her first job, which she has obtained through the help of Boas and Benedict. It is a post as Assistant Curator of Ethnology at the American Museum of Natural History, an affiliation she is to maintain, in various posts, her entire life.

The Museum will be her home. She is given a tiny attic room high up under its imposing roof. This niche under the eaves becomes her true home. "I felt secure," she says of her sanctuary, which had earlier been an apartment for the building's janitor and his family. "I would manage to stay there always." The room seems to be a lifelong refuge, a kind of Stone Age cave where she can escape from husbands and the public.

Now she finds she is a celebrity. Luther has been to Europe but Mead has lived among "savages."

At a dinner party the hostess asks her, "But do they have table manners?"

"They have finger bowls, Mrs. Ogburn."

At the Museum she rearranges the Maori collection, a task which does not demand too much time; her light schedule allows her to work on the manuscript of the book about Samoa. She also produces some shorter, more scientific papers for academic journals ("The Role of the Individual in Samoan Culture," "Social Organization of Manu'a" are examples). Luther, who has now left the ministry, is teaching anthropology, a subject in which he has no field experience. She remarks with what appears to be a touch of bitterness that she is a "resource" at breakfast, for Luther must draw her out about the subject for his courses.

In retrospect she labels the winter "odd." She is informed that she has a tipped uterus, and so cannot bear children. When she had married Luther she had thought of him as the future father of her children. Her dream of a life in a drafty old rectory with the Reverend Cressman and lots of children has fallen apart. She sees Luther as a failed minister, and seems to think little of him as a budding anthropologist. She can see no common goal with her husband, despite his shift in career. And her own life is obviously changed, for she cannot follow the role models of her grandmother and mother, of being wife and worker, slipping from one to another. A winter of unexpected demands and unpleasant surprises.

Mead is haunted by the question that arose when her ship docked at Marseilles, whether to stay with her husband, despite the lukewarm character of their marriage, or to throw in her life with Reo, brilliant and stormy as he is. She has taken the easy, the safe course. But the question remains with her. Coolly she tries to analyze the situation. Continuing with Luther as his wife could only be on the basis of "cooperation," a term she fails to explain over half a century later in discussing the dilemma in *Blackberry Winter.* But it is clear that to remain in her marriage would mean years and years of continued blandness. On the other hand, life with Reo offers challenges, excitement, opportunities to work together in the field.

As she mulls over the situation, following her career as an anthropologist but frustrated as a potential mother, as a woman, she comes to realize that she need not remain married to Luther. She faces a dilemma: Luther at home or the impetuous Reo, still at Cambridge, but only a few days away by ship. Luther or Reo? It looks to the faraway observer—and especially to her close friends and her relatives—as if she is making a coldhearted decision. With Luther a sense of shared purpose is being lost. With Reo she can have dreams of careers in common, even without children. She is nothing if not clearheaded throughout life.

But Reo, too, is having problems. He writes to Mead (they have kept up a running correspondence) that his teachers and he do not agree. They are respected men but he is having arguments with them. His ambition, as she had noted during the return from the Pacific, is pushing him hard. Reo wants to make his mark "immediately." He has changed fields from psychology to anthropology, but his work about dreams, *The Mind in Sleep*, has been published at his own cost. It does not receive a hearing in the scientific world.

Reo writes her again. He has received a grant from the

Australian National Research Council to do fieldwork and will go to Sydney later in the year. He will then continue on to New Guinea to study an obscure tribe called the Dobuans, a people much feared by their neighbors for their powers of black magic. Margaret and Reo set up a rendezvous in Europe.

Leaving Luther at home, she crosses the Atlantic by ship, ostensibly for a study of South Pacific materials in German museums, but actually to meet Reo. In *Blackberry Winter* she says little about the emotions involved in this secret tryst, whether she is anguished or guilty about the deception, or overjoyed at meeting the man who may become her second husband.

She sees that their relationship is still "tempestuous." Mead again faces the dilemma of her first meeting with Reo, but now it is condensed into unbearable tension, an unequal balance: One side of the scale is the almost plodding Luther, on the other an exciting, imaginative Reo, almost explosive with ideas for the future.

In recounting the event so many decades later, she seems cold, too analytical. One doesn't know the details of their intimate conversations—yet "when we parted I had agreed to marry him," she says in the fewest words possible. "I returned to New York to say good-bye to Luther."

Her head echoing with Reo's plans for the future, Mead puts the situation to Luther. He is agreeably pleasant. No stormy scenes are reported. No high emotion. In fact, he is almost too agreeable. It seems that he too has found someone else. The Margaret-Luther-Reo triangle quickly sorts itself out, the participants are realigning themselves, for now there are four people involved, and Luther will also remarry.

Everyone is understanding, so understanding that Mead and Luther can spend a quiet week together before he sails off to England to meet his future second wife. She will eventually bear him a child.

This is the end of Luther, though Mead can remark parenthetically in her autobiography that "he later became a first-rate archeologist, working in a discipline that brought into play all his skills with physical things as well as his human sensitivity. But that was later." One gets the impression that she is making an effort to be nice.

Family and friends are shocked by the quadrangle—Luther and his plans to remarry, Margaret and Reo and their plans. Divorce was still uncommon in the 1920's. "I found it difficult to bear the fact that most of my friends, when they had time to spare from their own complicated lives, were accusing me of heartlessness." She seems anguished by the accusations. But she has work to do, a manuscript to complete, a new marriage to enter into. She has to solve the details of getting together in a fortuitous place with Reo, who has now arrived among the Dobuans.

Reo's Dobuans—some forty souls in all—live on a primitive and remote island, Terewa. No one knows English, and from his second day Reo speaks no English whatever. "I had no interpreter," he remarks, "but acquired the language by contagion. At the end of three months nothing said passed over me, and nothing much in a quarrel with many shouting more or less simultaneously." It is dangerous work, and he is doing what few scientists have done (though traders and missionaries have often taken such chances), landing on an isolated cannibal island without a word of the native tongue and only a hearsay and inaccurate knowledge of what the people are like. Despite his high-strung emotions, Reo is also intelligent, courageous, intuitive and poetic, and he grasps the fearsome realities of Dobuan life, so enlivened by the frightening practices of sorcery. It is a trip untrammelled by aid, or even information, from any government official, and it is one of the few places untouched by missionaries. No outsider, black or white, has ever ventured to live among the Dobuans.

Terewa's high mountains, volcanic cones, bronzed rocks framed in the dense jungle overlooking bays and inlets of intensely clear blue water are picturesque scenes. But the mountains, though beautiful, are considered by the tribes on neighboring islands to be gloomy and treacherous—adjectives also applied to the Dobuans. A cloud of superstitious fear engulfs Terewa, for no outsider has dared approach its sandy shores. The Anglo-Polish anthropologist Bronislaw Malinowski, who had worked among the Trobriands, a few miles away across the strait, wrote that "the very name of Sewatupa [the main Terewan volcano] strikes terror into the heart" of all the other islanders.

The Dobuans eat both man and dog, and practice the most deadly witchcraft of all the islanders. They are mean and jealous, and dominate the entire area by their fearful raids: Entire canoe-loads of other islanders are known to have been captured and eaten by the Dobuans.

These frightening, mysterious people occupy five months of Reo's time on this, his first, expedition into the field. Yet he approaches them fearlessly. Immediately a strange myth springs up about the white stranger, though he is careful to dispose of it at once.

> I learned Dobuan quickly at the outset and made a journey across Fergusson Island [where the Dobuans obtained certain herbs for garden magic] speaking it, before rumour had gone across the Island announcing who I was or where I came from. One woman said I was the spirit of her dead brother come back from the dead. She prophesied, on this basis, a general resurrection of the dead shortly, and told everyone to kill all their pigs

and dogs. A wave of this superstition swept over the island and in several tribes the livestock, litters and all, were exterminated. The District Officer of the Administration tracked down the woman prophet who was partly responsible for the state of chaos that he found, livestock exterminated, no gardening being done, houses stored against a siege in fear of the coming resurrection of the spirits. He got her too late, after expectation had almost died and chaos was already changing back to normal routine.

A movement such as this, in which the indigenous people expected a savior of some kind, the expulsion of the whites, and the coming of many European goods for the islanders, was then known as a nativistic cult. These movements took dramatic turns, and at their height, immediately after World War II, they were called Cargo Cults.

Aside from whatever supernatural aspect the Dobuans find in Reo, they adopt him as a member of the Green Parrot clan, give him the personal name of a Green Parrot man of an earlier generation who died without any sister's children as heirs and provide him with land for a house. Reo thus joins the complicated kinship system, which is traced not from father to son, but from father's sister to the sister's son. Certain young people can now call him "my father," to which he replies, "my child."

Reo is also taught, grudgingly—but he is persistent—many charms and incantations employed in sorcery. Sorcery is the means par excellence of accomplishing virtually everything within Dobuan society. Gardens are planted according to charms and incantations, and other people's gardens destroyed also by charms and incantations. Men seduce women, and women seduce men, with the aid of magic (there can be no adult sexual relationship without sorcery). Charms, amulets, sacred stones, spittle, uneaten food, pieces of clothing, "personal leavings" (as Reo so delicately phrases it)—anything can be used against another person to gain one's own objectives. Nothing good or evil is attainable but through sorcery. Children begin to learn the charms and incantations at six or eight, and will grow up to be feared sorcerers.

Sorcery is "hot." The art requires, generates heat. When engaged in a magical rite, the sorcerer must keep his body hot and parched: He drinks salt water, abstains from food and chews ginger. Ginger is chewed to the accompaniment of many incantations, and is spat on the object of illness. It is chewed in all the incantations to ward off squalls at sea, and spat at the lowering winds. Ginger spat upon a canoe makes it seaworthy and speedy. The sight of a magician chewing ginger, spitting it at intervals on the object charmed and muttering his spell is a common one in Terewa. "Moreover," adds Reo, "there is believed to be virtue in ginger chewing alone—I saw men who were anxious to get a man who had just run amuck with a spear to chew ginger. I was engaged in deluging his body with cold water, while they were pressing ginger into his mouth—so there was some incompatibility between our theories."

It is lonely, dangerous work, but after five months Reo has accomplished a major task, the "functional" analysis of a difficult society—that is, how it functions, or works. Reo then visits the Basima, a neighboring tribe, staying a month with them. At last he returns to Australia to recuperate from the ordeals of jungle life. After three months at home, it is time for him to meet Mead, now on her way across the Pacific by ship.

The coming rendezvous has required much planning. It is not easy for two people in opposite sides of the world, in different hemispheres, to mesh marriage and career, especially in the light of jobs and other commitments. Mead, however, might be said to think on several levels at once. She has finished the manuscript of *Coming of Age in Samoa*—the book will appear while she is away, late in the fall of 1928—and she thus turns her attention to a field related to anthropology, one which she believes will enable her to meet Reo. She wants to do some research in psychology.

Under the influence of Sigmund Freud and his followers, especially the psychologists Lucien Lévy-Bruhl and Jean Piaget, many anthropologists have come to assume that "primitive" people and "civilized" children have much in common. It seems apparent to certain scientists that the adults in so-called backward societies are more or less on the level of children of advanced societies, being irrational, emotional, not particularly aware of logical deductions and conclusions, and that their unconscious minds function in similar ways. The mind of the "savage" and the mind of the child in the advanced culture, so the theory goes, are fairly close to each other in beliefs in nonsensical ideas: The savage's belief in myths and the supernatural roughly parallels the child's belief in fairy tales. But the child grows out of his "primitiveness." His mind develops and matures, while the savage's doesn't. Moreover, Freud had also said that both the child's mind and the savage's resemble that of the neurotic individual in certain ways.

The theory is interesting: On the surface it seems plausible, and some scientists have accepted it without careful analysis, and certainly without testing. Mead would like to test it. She is intrigued by Freud's three-part balance of savage, civilized child and neurotic, and she would like to carry the theory a step further. If primitive adults resemble the children of the Westernized, advanced nations in their mental processes and the unconscious (an assumption no one has proven, of course), what is the thinking of primitive children like?

Mead writes two articles dealing with Freud's hypothesis concerning the behavioral patterns of primitive people, "An Ethnologist's Footnote to Totem and Taboo" and "A Lapse of Animism among a Primitive People." She points out that the kind of experience that the Freudians postulate as common throughout the world—that all adolescents go through a period of "storm and stress"—does not appear among the Samoan girls she has studied. To her the issue seems to be an important one. Nothing has been done on it, and she wants to pursue it further by studying an even younger group, pre-adolescent children in an even more primitive society.

The research could be done almost anywhere, but since Reo is in the New Guinea area with the Dobuans, she leaves the choice of location up to him. He decides on the Admiralty Islands, an archipelago off the northeast coast of New Guinea. The complicated details are worked out between New York and New Zealand. Grants are obtained— Reo gets one from the Australian National Research Council, and Margaret the Social Science Research Council, a U.S. organization.

She travels alone across the Pacific by ship. At Auckland, New Zealand, Reo boards her boat. They have not seen each other for over a year, not since their secret rendezvous in Germany. Impetuous but not tempestuous, Reo demands that she marry him then, at that moment, instead of waiting until the ship docks at Sydney, as they had originally planned. Off to the registry office they rush, only at the last minute getting a ring small enough for her finger. But married they

are and they return to the boat just in time for its sailing.
Frustrating months of waiting have suddenly been dissolved.
Ahead lies "a professional partnership in field work with
Reo."

Growing Up with Reo

NOW JOINED IN MARRIAGE AND careers, Margaret and Reo, on shipboard, glide over placid seas, stopping at Sydney, where more passengers and freight are taken aboard. Then they steam northward toward New Guinea.

These are waters of unknown histories, for the peoples are primitive and have no written record, and tribal legends could be based on events a decade back or a thousand years before. But these deep blue waters have seen the migrations of unknown races on daring canoe trips, tiny groups of people brave enough to sail into the unknown. And, in far more recent times, Captain James Cook had sailed these same waters, discovering the New Hebrides chain to the distant east, and Australia and New Zealand, now to the south. After Cook had come the Dutch, French, Spaniards and Germans, claiming lands, founding colonies. Magellan had once gone through these waters, losing men and ships, but succeeding in making the first voyage around the world. Traders and beachcombers, missionaries, planters, slavers (the notorious blackbirders) had ravaged the islands in search of riches, coconut, sandalwood, cheap labor for the plantations of Australia and Peru, souls for the various churches. Ships had foundered and crews been lost; men and women had died of starvation, wounds, fevers, in cannibal feasts in these islands. It was a wild, savage area, picturesque as a postcard but often hostile, deadly.

Soon their ship rounds the southeast point of New Guinea, with its treacherous straits and reefs and mountainous jungled islands, and lands at Rabaul, on the adjoining island of New Britain.

All of the New Guinea Territory has been a favored field for anthropologists, for its many tribes show widely differing cultures and characteristics. The very wildness and isolation of the great island and its many offshore archipelagos and island clusters have produced hundreds of small tribal and clan groups, with unrelated languages, customs, myths and legends and religions. Even with European colonization, the region, in the late 1920's when Mead and her husband arrive to study, is, except for certain areas, virtually untouched by white influence.

Margaret and Reo find Rabaul a charming little tropical town, lying under the shadow of three threatening volcanoes, the Mother, the North Daughter and the South Daughter. Rabaul had been founded only as recently as 1910 by the Germans. (Much of the New Guinea Territory had been first a German colony, and after World War I ended in 1918, the islands had been administered primarily by Australia.) Rabaul is neatly laid out, resembling a garden more than the administrative center of one of the most important of the Pacific colonies. It is a center for a small population of white officials, traders and planters, for it is the only town with any kind of Western amenities. Though in the heart of an area overwhelmingly native, it is a solidly European town, ruled by whites through a native police force, whose members are recruited from dozens of different tribes.

Shortly after Mead and Fortune pass through Rabaul the police—called "boys" by the whites—go on strike, paralyzing the administration. Many of the police have come from a northern island called Manus, one of the Admiralty chain of the territory, and these islanders are among the strike leaders.

The strike is crucial in white-native relations, for in place of the sporadic outbreaks by people in the bush which the local district administrators put down easily, the police strike takes place in the very heart of the government, and is well planned and well executed. The main issue is one of wages, along with the manner in which whites treat the natives (a strike on another island is called the Dog Movement, because the people believe that they are treated as dogs by the whites). Led by the boss-boys, many of whom are from Manus, the police lead the entire indigenous labor force out of Rabaul to the relative safety of the Catholic and Protestant missions. Eventually the strike is crushed by the government; the police and the workers do not receive any better wages, but the natives have learned that they can defy the white man.

The strike is at that time outside of Mead's own work, but one of the leaders, whom she does not meet at Rabaul, is a man named Paliau. He is to play a role in her work some twenty-five years later. Meanwhile the young couple make preparations for their field trip.

Reo has decided on the basis of advice given in Australia by anthropologists there that the Admiralty Islands would be a fertile area for study, because no modern ethnological research has been done in them. He has further narrowed down the area to Manus, home of some of the police-boys, after a talk with an officer in the New Guinea Service whom he had met in Sydney. The choice of village where they are to work, Peré (or Peri), comes about because a government official at Rabaul "lends" him a schoolboy from that village to teach him and Mead the language. The boy, Bonyalo, is not happy about leaving this poinsettia- and orchid-filled tropical metropolis, with its many attractions, to return to his primitive village, but he has to acquiesce to orders.

The inter-island steamer brings them first to Lorengau, the government station on the Admiralties. Mead writes home that "There are some two dozen white people" at the post. "Everyone speaks to everyone else and hate is rampant. It was really better at Pago Pago where they didn't speak to each other." She describes the few officials, the missionaries, the traders and planters, some of whom are Chinese or Japanese, and adds: "Such flimsy structures of a hundred or so white men govern and exploit this vast country—find gold, plant great plantations, trade for shell, hide their failures in other lands, drink inordinately, run into debt, steal each other's wives, go broke and commit suicide or get rich—if they know how."

After ten days at Lorengau getting ready for the final leg of their voyage, Margaret and Reo, with their guides Manuwai and Bonyalo, sail off in a seagoing canoe to the distant village of Peré, where they will spend six months in fieldwork. It is midnight when they arrive in the village's moonlit lagoon, hungry and tired. The next morning they immediately go to work photographing the people.

The Great Admiralty Archipelago (as it is formally called) is about sixty miles long; it is made up of some forty islands in all, but the land mass totals only sixty square miles. The sea, rather than the land, is the prime source of livelihood for many of the people, especially the Manus, the most compact of the three major tribes inhabiting the islands. Of the other two, the Mantankor are also a canoe people, while the Usiai have a way of life that depends more on the land than the water. When Margaret and Reo land, the estimated population is about 13,000 people.

Reo Fortune

In Peré, Margaret Mead wears a costume worn by widows on Manus. The beadwork is obtained before death by the husband and the woman's male relatives after extended bargaining. Many factors—the hard life, dangers at sea, even sorcery—contribute to the early death of men and women alike in Manus and other South Pacific cultures.

The entire area is wildly primitive and barely out of the Stone Age cannibalism that the Germans had encountered when they had taken the Admiralties over as a colony. Until 1926 no white had ever entered the densely wooded interior of the main island. The people had not taken easily to white rule, and the whites had responded with punitive measures, in some cases killing off rebelling islanders.

Mead finds that the Manus (the people have the same name as their island) have only a superficial resemblance to the Samoans she had studied. The Manus, unlike the Samoans, live over the water, building their thatch-roofed houses on stilts along the shallows of the lagoon. Also, the Manus are not Polynesians, like the Samoans, but Melanesians, a dark-skinned people related to the vast family of Negro and Negroid groups of the tropical belt. Mead notes that until 1912, when they were pacified by the German administration, war had been one of their major, enjoyable preoccupations. She has come at a time when the Manus have shifted to another kind of economy: With war denied them as a means of gathering wealth, the Manus have, for the past few years, concentrated on voyaging and trading, practices that have become passions, ways of life and pastimes. The Manus are people of the shrewdest type, and their entire lives are centered around the accumulation of wealth, its display and its conspicuous consumption.

Mead finds Peré an idyllic setting: a great lagoon, waving palms, distant mountains, the roar of the open sea beyond the reefs, the canoes gliding gracefully about, children playing, people fishing. But, she says, despite the tropical beauty which so appeals to the visitor, "we shared in the local attitudes." To the Manus the reef is a constant threat, the mountains foreboding, haunted with spirits and ghosts. There is no dancing at night, as with the Samoans. Moralistic and avenging spirits will strike down evildoers. "The whole society is run by the spirits of the immediate ancestors, who preserve exceedingly human characteristics—easily angered, easily solaced. Each house has a special guardian spirit of the owner's father or uncle and this spirit both punishes and protects," she writes home.

At first Mead thinks the Manus are "a gay and open-hearted people . . . friendly in feeling, though unmannerly," but she later revises her opinion of the villagers, for the society seems rather oppressive. The young women are kept indoors, and the young men paddle aimlessly about the lagoon, with little to occupy their thoughts and time. For the two anthropologists there is little chance for play and relaxation in this ambiguous atmosphere; they concentrate on their research. "It's as delightful a place as we could have found in New Guinea," she says at first, only to correct this impression by saying later, it is "a hard-working life with almost no pleasures."

Margaret and Reo set about learning the language, which is but one of twenty in the Admiralties. It is enormously difficult, with sounds hard to pronounce, and a great amount of individual variation, but soon they can carry on simple conversations, and within a short time are able to do their research entirely in Manus, even making their notes in it.

For a few days Margaret and Reo live in a small house kept by the Australian government for its officials on tour, but then they have a house of their own constructed on the edge of the village. They have a host of child servants, a cook-boy and some teenage girls who are supposed to do the laundry but, since they must not be seen by certain males in Peré because of tribal taboos, are often hiding. After an initial enthusiasm for the food ("Food had turned out to be much better than we had dared to hope"), the diet is soon reduced to smoked fish and taro, a tasteless root, and occasionally a wild duck or pigeon shot by Reo.

Peré village is small—210 people in sixty-three households—but there are, for Mead's work, eighty-seven children under the age of puberty, or right at it. The small size of the village and the simplicity of Manus society make study easy for her. She goes about her work methodically, observing each child in detail in its play and home life, recording not only what the child itself does but all the details of family relationships, the number of children in a marriage and their whereabouts, how the marriage was financed and by whom (for fathers and uncles finance the weddings of younger men and spend much wealth in doing so). Both the men and the women in the household are questioned about their relationship with the guardian spirits—does the man have powers of divination (that is, can he talk to the spirits)? and is the woman a medium? The children, of course, are growing up very differently from children in Western households, and Mead wants to know when they were weaned, if they chew betel nut (a kind of narcotic) or pepper leaves, or if they smoke, if they wear clothing, urinate in public, can dance, can paddle a canoe, who are their companions and what games are played.

All the Manus children, no matter what age, are inveterate smokers and beg constantly for tobacco. To preserve their supplies, Reo smokes his pipe only late at night, and Margaret risks an occasional cigarette. Both the young anthropologists suffer from malaria—Mead estimates later that she was ill a third of the time at Manus. But the work goes on.

She wants the children to draw, seemingly a universal custom. It is, one would think, a part of a child's life in every culture. Drawing is a useful tool not only for the teacher but for the ethnologist, for it shows how the child views the world. Drawings also reflect what the child is learning and absorbing from peers, older children, parents and other models, as well as from teachers. But the Manus children have never drawn. "I found, contrary to all expectations, that these 'primitive

Margaret Mead's second husband, Reo Fortune, the brilliant but controversial anthropologist, accompanies her on the lengthy field trip to Manus. Reo is seated on the edge of the lagoon where Peré village is, with one of the ever-present children who follow Reo and Mead wherever they go.

children' showed not a trace of the easy animism of our own children, who draw men in the moon and houses with faces."

So Mead patiently teaches the Manus children, starting with those at puberty, and working down to the youngest, the use of colors and surfaces. Normally a hundred drawings will give an anthropologist basic clues to a culture, but she must collect 35,000 from the children before she is satisfied that she has understood the situation correctly. She finds that the children depict only the most literal representations of what she points out to them as possible subjects. There is no free play of the imagination. So her research convinces her that there is no natural animism among the Manus youngsters.

Nor does animism enter into the adults' religious life. Unlike many cultures, that of the Manus has a very simple religious system, one based on household spirits, each family being supervised by the spirit of a recently deceased male member. This spirit—"Sir Ghost" is the term Mead is to use later in her *New Lives for Old*—stimulates and chastises, protects and defends. Sexual standards, especially for the women, are extremely strict, and the Manus believe that all sickness is a punishment by the household spirit for either sexual or economic sins. Margaret and Reo learn to greet the news of an islander's illness not with a question about the nature of the disease but with what spirit is involved.

Manus life, the anthropologists realize, is strict, puritanical and not very creative. The children have shown there is little instinctive religious feeling, and no natural art. There is, in fact, no art at all in Manus culture, no artifacts, none of the great wooden statues and masks and carvings on houses and boats that so distinguish other Pacific tribes. The Manus are culturally barren, though neighboring tribes are superlative artists and create numerous articles of great beauty—war clubs, ceramics and bark cloth among them. Whatever art the

Manus possess comes from trading with other groups. They have much wealth as the result of constantly exchanging with inland tribes, always to their own advantage, trading artifacts back and forth to increase their economic and social standing. Their houses are filled with wooden objects, large slit gongs, carved platform beds, dagger handles, wooden bowls and scoops, human figures of all sizes, and numbers of beautifully made pots obtained from neighboring peoples. Why waste time on something you can get easily in trade? is the Manus attitude. Their food comes from daily fishing and periodic expeditions to onshore villages to get carbohydrate foods.

In the 1920's the traditional currencies of dogs' teeth and shell money, along with pigs as an item of barter on specialized occasions, are still in use; shillings obtained in work for foreigners are valued mostly as a means of getting more dogs' teeth. Dogs' teeth exhibit the same characteristics in the South Pacific islands as gold or silver currency in the rest of the world. The scarcity of dogs (as of gold) gives the currency more value.

The former German administration of New Guinea and the Bismarck Archipelago had come close to destroying the local economies at Manus and elsewhere; the Kaiser's officials had imported dogs' teeth from China and Turkey (where they had had no value at all), causing a rate of inflation of 800 to 1,000 percent. The price for a bride, Mead notes, is now 10,000 dogs' teeth, where 1,000 had been standard before German rule. The Germans had further devalued the dogs' teeth by introducing artificial—counterfeit—teeth made of synthetics, thus causing even more inflation. After this disastrous depression of currency in the German-administered areas, World War I had brought an end to the importation of fake dogs' teeth (and incidentally a crippling inflation in paper money in Germany, which one might have attributed to avenging South Pacific spirits). The artificial teeth now developed into a valued commodity since the supply had ceased. A simple lesson in elementary economics.

In the long run, however, all such currency as dogs' teeth, shells and beads are to lose all value except ceremonially, as Western monies come to predominate in the area. Many islanders become indentured laborers in order to earn the hard currency with which to buy the European goods they are soon persuaded to desire, such as steel knives, saws, mirrors, watches, lanterns, lockboxes, clothing, flashlights, beer, alcohol, cigarettes and all kinds of trinkets.

The Manus of the 1920's have no strong political system. There are no chiefs or headmen as in most primitive cultures, though there is a rough semblance of rank. The men in control are the financial leaders, each of whom is a nucleus for several lesser men who merely fish and feed their families. Village political life is based on a complex system of exchanges on an "affinal" (or marriage-related) basis, imperishable valuables obtained in other trades being traded again for food, ceramics, grass skirts and other items of daily use. The shrewd men among the Manus are able to increase their wealth in the constant bartering; the less businesslike fail to advance.

The Manus are a simple, primitive example of the laws of supply and demand, of the accumulation of property, of the power of wealth. Every Manus man is constantly stimulated to increase his holdings; a few succeed but others remain "middle-income" or poor, as in many societies not only in the West but in more complex parts of Asia and Africa.

There is much pressure on individuals and their families in the endless struggle for more wealth. Consequently everyone is active, and family and business ties are strong. But this activity, and the power that wealth brings, works best for the older, successful men. The young men are often quite dependent upon wealthy seniors who underwrite their marriages—always costly—and thus become dominant over the helpless juniors and entangle them in protracted economic exchanges. Only by becoming a ruthless trader himself can a man escape such involvement.

Many younger men leave the islands to work for Europeans, or join the police-boys. An Australian report summed up the precariousness of the situation of the Manus by remarking:

> Never have I met a people so individualistic. . . . Every man is jealous of his property rights and privileges however great or small. [Differences of] wealth and poverty . . . are seldom so apparent as in Manus. It is for this reason that one meets so many Manus men who leave their homes to work for non-natives and who never wish to return. They are the poor, and poverty means no standing in the community and no wife.

Margaret and Reo do not react to the Manus in the same manner. Still carrying memories of his recent stay among the Dobuans, so hostile and dour and involved in their sorcery, suspicious of each other and of neighbors and strangers alike, Reo finds the Manus by comparison open and friendly, though at first he suspects they are holding back information as the Dobuans had. But, in fact, the Manus have no information to keep secret. Mead, after her stay with the easygoing Samoans, sees the Manus as puritanical, materialistic, driven people who are prey to unseen forces eager to punish them for the least transgression or misdemeanor. But their varying views of the people create no problems between them. Instead they have a good-natured rivalry, which the Manus enjoy, in amassing specimens of artifacts, Mead for the Museum of Natural History, Reo for the Sydney Museum.

The work among the Manus takes six months, a short period for a field trip. Mead has often been accused of hasty research by some of her colleagues, but she makes the point in *Growing Up in New Guinea* that in a simple society such as the Manus, the trained investigator can do the necessary work quickly. "The cultural tradition is simple enough to be almost entirely contained within the memory of an average adult member of society. . . . With the immense superiority over the native of being able to record in writing each aspect of the culture as it is learned, the anthropologist is in an excellent position for research within a comparatively short time." She adds that an equally isolated village in a Western land is far more difficult to study than a primitive one, for it would be affected by "echoes and fragments from a hundred different kinds of cultural elaboration." A primitive village of the types she has been studying in the Pacific would have a few basic patterns, but an American town, drawing upon half the world, with numerous types of family structure, religions, ways of bringing up children, of viewing life, of marriage and work, of daily interests, is far more complex, and in effect can offer an infinite field of study for the anthropologist, one that can never be fully completed, for Western life is endlessly changing.

Decades later, Mead, more mature and more experienced, retracts this rather boastful view of her ability to grasp an entire culture, even a simple one, in so short a period. By 1953 she "calculated that it would take some thirty years of continuous observation to document the whole Manus repertoire, and Manus is not a very complex culture."

But the Manus study has been done, wonderfully complete, she believes, in a very short time, the precious notebooks and rolls of film carefully wrapped, the last exchange of tobacco and presents made with the villagers. The Manus consider their departure an act for mourning. The death drums are taken out and their deep mournful rumbling begins. The canoe is loaded, and Margaret and Reo wade through the edge of the surf and climb aboard. Pokanau, who has been Reo's chief informant, makes a farewell speech. The drums beat on.

Off the canoe goes, the drums dying away in the roar of the surf. The Manus have no way of knowing Mead's world; their horizons are limited: Rabaul, the most they know of the outside world, beyond the edge of the sea, and Sydney, a rare dream entered upon by but a few daring men. Mead knows the Manus will never see her book, view her photographs. They are completely illiterate, and they believe that she will be swallowed by the ocean. For her part, she assumes that they are a dying society, to be engulfed by the encroaching shapeless mass of Westernization, to become just another Pacific proletariat, rootless, without power, forgetting the slim culture that sustained them over the unrecorded centuries.

The two anthropologists are soon in civilized Rabaul, their six months of Manus life fading away into a collection of notes and photographic images. At Rabaul Reo leaves his wife to return to the Dobuans for a short period to take pictures for his projected book.

Mead stays in Rabaul with a woman named Phebe Parkinson, the wife of a now-deceased German adventurer named Richard Parkinson, a famous character of the South Pacific. Phebe Parkinson is half-American, half-Samoan, and is a mine of information about local customs and history, as well as current gossip. Phebe tells Mead about the problems of an English anthropologist named Gregory Bateson, who is living alone in the New Guinea jungle making a study of the Baining, an isolated tribe in eastern New Britain.

"Poor Mr. Bateson," says Phebe Parkinson, "didn't eat right and got those terrible tropical ulcers."

Reo returns from the Dobuans, his photographic work completed. Now a conflict arises between Mead and her husband. Even though he has been granted a fellowship at Columbia University, Reo would prefer for both of them to go to New Zealand to live. But since he has no prospects of a job in his own country, he believes that he would have to work as a laborer. Giving up a fellowship in favor of manual work might be romantic, but, Mead writes, it was an idea "that I had enough sense not to undertake."

On the other hand, she worries that life in a land—her own country—where Reo would be a stranger and where she would be well known because of the success of *Coming of Age in Samoa* (which she has learned is doing well) would be uncomfortable for him. Her common sense wins out: It will be New York rather than New Zealand. They board the ship for the long trip to the States.

At San Francisco Mead is operated on for an undisclosed problem—"something [during the operation] went wrong and I almost died," she remarks. She is weak, and the train trip across America is something of a nightmare for her. But in New York her friends tell her what she has learned by letter, that she is a celebrity because of *Coming of Age in Samoa.* The famous author and her unfamous husband take a brownstone on 102nd Street off Broadway in Manhattan, halfway between Columbia, where Reo is to study, and the Museum of Natural History, where Mead is to resume her job.

Coming of Age in Samoa has become a best-seller. With the kind of fortuitous good luck that marks most of her life, young Mead has selected an area and a community where her special talents might go to work. Her own background—the intelligent, academic family, her Grandma Mead's special tutoring, her education, strange as it has been, her self-possession, her ability to adapt to a totally unfamiliar world, one with strange customs, food, language and housing, with remarkable ease—has helped in the task. If she had selected the declining native culture of the Tuamotu archipelago, her first choice, one must doubt that she would have produced so successful a book, for the exotic background and the frank reporting of sexual freedom of Samoan teenagers (though her language is quite proper by today's standards), helped popularize *Coming of Age*. Secondly, because others had already thoroughly explored the more technical aspects of Samoan culture, such as language, clan structure and mythology, she was free to explore the completely overlooked area of the maturing Samoan woman.

The book is unlike anything published before by a trained anthropologist. As some reviewers pointed out (and some academics objected), she brought a novelist's skill and insights to bear upon her subjects. She was uncommonly gifted in the art of expressing her observations and ideas in clear and graphic English, simply and descriptively, with a maximum of information in a minimum number of words.

Mead remarks later that it is the first such work written by a serious professional for the educated layman in which no effort was made to impress one's colleagues in the academic world. She was not trying to score "theoretical points" over her fellow professionals, but was arguing for "the future of young people, who in the United States were becoming less than they might be because we understood so little about what a difference a culture can make, in terms of stress and strains, in individual fulfillment or defeat." The important people to reach, she says, are not the academics but "teenagers and those just escaped from adolescence, who would soon be parents determining the shape of the world for their children."

Coming of Age in Samoa is soon accepted as standard reading in the human or "behavioral" sciences, as well as a best-
seller, as Americans become more and more conscious of the
stresses of modern living upon the young.

Mead's father, who had a book about agricultural economics appear at the same time ("a stimulating contribution" and
"a sensible discussion" were typical reviewers' comments),
told her she would never again write a book as good as *Coming of Age in Samoa*, because "as I grew older and wiser, I
would 'know too much,' and the books would inevitably be
harder to read. I believed this for a while, until a European
psychoanalyst told me that when he read the book he believed it to have been written by a very old lady."

The reviews were mixed, the popular and general publications tending to accept it uncritically, and the academics
finding things to complain about, however, without challenging the core of the book itself. "A fascinating view of pagan
girlhood . . . keen insight and a thorough knowledge of her
subject" were key phrases in the review by H.F.M. in the
Boston Transcript. "An extraordinarily subtle performance,"
said an unsigned review in *Bookmaster.* "Frank, with the
clean, clear frankness of the scientist, unbiased in its judgment, richly readable in its style," said *The New York Times.*
Mead's friend Ruth Benedict was unusually busy with reviews, for in *The New Republic* she stated that *Coming of Age
in Samoa* was challenging not only to the educator and to the
parent of growing children but also to the anthropological
student of psychological problems among primitive people,
and that "It is a book for which we have been waiting." In the
Journal of Philosophy Dr. Benedict thought it was an "excellent ethnological picture of an alien culture."

The academics were harder. In the *American Anthropologist*, R.H. Lowrie said, "On some points made by Dr. Mead
I must frankly avow skepticism. It is hard to believe that all

but the youngest boys and girls should fail to use ordinary kinship terms correctly; or, in an absolute way, that Samoan children do not learn to work through learning to play." Even so, Lowrie liked her methods of working and thought other people would soon copy them. The noted anthropologist Robert Redfield was more critical. "For all the intimate association with Samoans the book is somehow disappointing. There are exceedingly interesting pages," he said, "but Miss Mead is interested, one feels, in problems and cases, not in human nature. There is no warmth in her account." Nels Anderson in *Survey* was also critical. "If this is intended to be a work of art, then the 'gay spirit' and Dr. Mead's impressionistic style are in place. If it is science, the book is somewhat of a disappointment. It lacks documental base." And so Mead learns the pleasures of a best-seller and the hazards of having it reviewed by academics.

Whatever the critical reaction, her six months in Polynesia are to have a profound effect upon the thinking of many Americans for much of the twentieth century. She writes some long, specialist scientific articles for the professional journals, but it is the popular version of her experiences that affects the public's thinking, not only about so-called primitive peoples and their cultures, but even certain aspects of American life, for Mead has added two chapters dealing with parallel problems in America to her graphic details of Samoa. The subtitle (not repeated in some of the many editions) is "A Psychological Study of Primitive Youth for Western Civilization." In the library journals it is categorized as "Samoa—Social life and customs. Adolescence. Sex (psychology)."

So far as Samoa is concerned, Mead can answer the question posed by Boas, who sent her on her trip: that of the inevitable storms and stresses of adolescence. They aren't universal but are culturally caused.

What makes growing up in Samoa so easy, so lacking in

stress? Is it the general casualness of Samoan life, despite the formalities of etiquette and custom? No one aims too high (nor too low)—no one shoots a little farther as Mead the Sagittarian does.

Mead notes the lack of deep feeling, of the high emotion that can stand out so strongly in the more highly motivated Americans. A median level is the standard for Samoan culture; the gifted being is held back until the mediocre can catch up, for the Samoans see their lives in terms of all the people rather than of the individual, as is the American ideal.

Mead can also find factors in Samoan society that ensure "nervous stability" among people. From the earliest ages Samoans are firsthand witnesses to birth, sex, pregnancy, death and the decay of the body. No Samoan child feels guilty about witnessing events commonplace in themselves, which are so often kept from the sight of the growing American. In fact, these events are so much a part of daily life that their calm acceptance allows an absence of neurosis, she believes. And adjustment in marriage is rarely difficult because of the intimacies of teenagers when growing up. But it is not merely a free expression in sex that produces the easygoing patterns of Samoan life, but the entire process, which makes no heavy demands on individuals except for those of the royal families, pushes no one to "achieve" whether or not he or she is capable of better effort. There is none of the adolescent storm and stress in Samoa that is so obvious in America.

But why does it happen in America? Her chapters about her own country tackle the very point that Boas had raised. Mead wants to make the difference clear, and draws simple parallels between the two societies; since *Coming of Age in Samoa* there have been many analyses of what has gone wrong with the American psyche, but what is interesting is that Mead put the problem into perspective so graphically in 1928, in terms that read as if written today.

In America, with its numerous standards and choices, adults strive desperately to bind their own children to courses which they themselves have chosen. The child may often resort to "devious and non-reputable means" to escape beliefs, practices, courses of action that have been pressed upon him or her.

> In our ideal picture of the freedom of the individual and the dignity of human relations, it is not pleasant to realise that we have developed a form of family organisation which often cripples the emotional life, and warps and confuses the growth of many individuals' power to consciously live their own lives.

America, she admits, is in a period of transition. Nevertheless

> we pay heavily for our heterogeneous, rapidly changing civilisation; we pay in high proportions of crime and delinquency, we pay in the conflicts of youth, we pay in an ever-increasing number of neuroses, we pay in the lack of a coherent tradition without which the development of art is sadly handicapped.

In the end, what Mead asks for, in the light of the many gains we have made, and can make, is freedom for individual choice and universal toleration which a heterogeneous culture, not a single, simple society like Samoa, alone can attain. Since America has the knowledge of many ways, she asks, why not leave our children free to choose among them?

It was this openness in talking to American adults, as much as her descriptions of the amatory intrigues of Samoan adolescents, that made *Coming of Age in Samoa* such a popular, controversial work, and gave it the long life it has enjoyed. New editions, in hardcover and paperback, continue to appear. It has been translated into many languages, studied in thousands of classrooms and read by many hundreds of thousands of people, including the children and grandchildren of her Samoans, curious about the ways in which their mothers and aunts and grandparents grew up on Tau.

While *Coming of Age in Samoa* is gaining fame and sales, Mead immerses herself in her other projects. Always a person of endless energy, she handles a full-time job at the American Museum of Natural History as Assistant Curator for Ethnology, and finishes the manuscript of her book about the Manus, working very quickly and easily. The entire process of publication, from writing to typesetting and production, requires barely more than a year from the time she and Reo return to New York, and the book appears in the fall of 1930. As a concession to popular ignorance, she calls the work *Growing Up in New Guinea*, for she suspects that few people would be knowledgeable enough to be attracted to a title that included the obscure name of Manus or of the Admiralty Islands. Reo, however, does not work so fiercely as his wife. He is still struggling with his book about the sorcerers of Dobu, and has not yet touched his massive pile of notes about the Manus.

Mead is almost compulsive about getting her fieldwork into print quickly. She complains how often anthropologists, including the most famous, let their material accumulate, eventually reaching the point where they are overwhelmed by notes that never get transcribed, much less published. She has realized from the beginning of her studies that fieldwork is useless unless the results can be placed before some kind of an audience.

The Manus book, effortlessly written, and like *Coming of Age in Samoa* almost novelistic in approach, is one of her better works. (Isidor Schneider, writing in *The New Republic,* commented that it is "an even more interesting book than Miss Mead's widely and deservedly praised *Coming of Age in Samoa.*") Mead is quite conscious of the work's narrative qualities and the fact that it avoided academic jargon. In an appendix, she stated that it seemed "advisable to couch . . . the language . . . outside the realm of controversy—in the field of the novelist—in order that it may be intelligible when some of the present dialectic points and their terminology have been outmoded. Such a course has the additional advantage of making the material more accessible to students from other fields."

Her Manus are not the easygoing, uncomplicated islanders that the Samoans are, but people very much like Americans, hard-driving, success-oriented, somewhat puritanical in their outlook, especially in sexual matters, and conscious of wealth and its uses. In contrast to many cultures in which peoples work and live cooperatively as clans or tribes, among the Manus it is the individual who is important, whose aggrandizement of wealth and power takes precedence to loyalty and the social well-being of the village or tribal group.

Throughout the book she can connect the Manus to Americans. It might be argued that not all Americans are as she sees them, but her strictures do have a broad relevance. She finds that both Manus and American children grow up untrammelled, with little respect for elders, custom and the niceties of life, spoiled beyond measure and at times even feared by their parents. Both grow up without responsibilities, thanks to the labor of those who make these long years of play possible, but who receive abuse rather than thanks from their children. In both cultures the business of making a living is more important than the conduct of life as an art. The ideal Manus man has no time for play; he is always up early doubling his strings of shell beads and dogs' teeth.

Today her comparison of Manus and Americans seems as if she had written it recently instead of half a century ago. The narrow-minded parents of the 1920's and the somewhat rebellious young she describes in her summary chapters that deal primarily with America are still with us, except that yesterday's rebels are now today's narrow-minded grandparents. The generation gap is wide, she feels, and children and parents are worlds apart. Manus children, she says, and American children are as a rule very lightly disciplined and taught very little respect for their elders. Neither society instills respect for age or knowledge, courtesy or kindness for elders. Neither teaches the children to work (as the Samoans do).

> Our children are given years of cultural non-participation in which they are permitted to live in a world of their own. They are allowed to say what they like, when they like, how they like, to ignore many of the conventions of their adults.

The American emphasis on the latest fads, the newest gadgets and most of all upon money as the basic standard produce

> a society very much like the Manus, an efficient, well-equipped, active society in which wealth is the only goal, and what a man has is substituted for what he is.

People are pigeonholed by what they have, and the pigeonholes are "very dull ones, houses, automobiles, clothes, all turned out wholesale." The individual himself, as a person, is not considered.

> Wealth is separable from age, from sex, from wit or beauty, from manners or morals. Once it becomes valued as a way of life, there is no respect for those things which must be learned, must be experienced to be understood. . . . In Manus as in America, life is not viewed as an art which is learned, but in terms of things which can be acquired. Those who have acquired them can command those who have not.

The indictment continues in detail. Mead wants Americans (she offers no cure for the Manus) to shift their values from having to being. The core of the problem lies with the elders, who of course have been conditioned by their elders; the youth will perpetuate the problem; "they [will] take over the adult life sullenly, with dull resentment." She is not optimistic in this book, though she becomes so in others, particularly when she is one of the elders. But now

> To treat our children as the Manus do, permit them to grow up as the lords of an empty creation, despising the adults who slave for them so devotedly, and then apply the whip of shame to make them fall in line with a course of life which they have never been taught to see as noble or dignified—this is giving a stone to those who have a right to good bread.

Her discoveries about the similarities between Manus and America receive a mixed reception. Isidor Schneider (of *The New Republic*) remarks that "If the book had appeared as a modern *Gulliver's Travels*, the description of Manus society would have sounded like a bitter satire on American life." In the *New York World* Harry Hansen writes, "Some of Miss Mead's criticism is superficial, but much of it goes deep. Miss Mead senses the holes in our culture, the deficiencies in our individual life." Ruth Benedict, writing for *Books*, gives an uncritical summary, perhaps because she was disappointed yet did not want to hurt her close friend. "The book is non-technical and easy to read," she says, and points out that the research was done mostly in the native language.

The academic views are far more critical. A typical one is by Nels Anderson, in the little-known *Survey*, who prefers her facts to her opinions.

> Dr. Mead is strongest in this study when she is present-ing her anthropological data. To me she is most inter-esting and informing when she stays with the concrete materials, with what they do and say in Manus. Just so, she is least convincing when she essays her educational comparisons. The final three chapters put her in the position of the man who tells a story and then bores us with explaining the point which was obvious all the while. These many references to the American father, what he does do and what he does not do, are neither wholly true nor wholly false.

But in the end, Mead's perceptions carry the book. In style and content, *Growing Up in New Guinea* stands on a level with *Coming of Age in Samoa*. Both books have helped her state her views on America. One feels in reading both, and thinking about her analyses of American life and culture, that she is not quite sure what she wants for her own country, for she is comparing the most highly evolved, technological soci-ety ever developed with two extremely simple, primitive, almost archaic, worlds. She can admire the informality and freedom of the Samoan teenager, with untrammelled sexual expression and the lack of guilt, though the adults conform to a strict hierarchy of social values, and lament the chaotic, materialistic Manus village so guilt-ridden because of its dependence on unseen ghosts and spirits. One senses that she would like to get America pinned down to a six-month study that can be neatly and deftly summarized in a third work. But this can never happen, because throughout her analyses of what is wrong with her country is the realization that it encompasses the complexity of ten thousand, a hundred thousand primitive societies and this very complexity almost defies definition.

While Mead is finishing her book on the Manus, the success of her *Coming of Age in Samoa* brings conflicts in her relations with Reo, still wrestling with the Dobuan magicians. They read each other's works at night—Mead is also involved in articles about the Manus—and each appreciates and criticizes what the other has done, but aside from this regular exhibition of professionalism, their household is "rather tempestuous." Each day with Reo seems like a battle.

At first the couple have no money, and only Mead has a job, a mere $2,500 a year, which is soon reduced because of the depression the nation is experiencing. Reo, with his fellowship at Columbia, earns nothing at all, and this adds to the tension. Then, the difficulties of a cross-national marriage— between a New Zealander, accustomed to a society where men usually have the say, and an American woman, accustomed to speaking out—increase the strain. "In addition," she says, "Reo did not like to see me doing the housework, which he did not intend to help me with"—because that was something New Zealand men did not do—"yet he felt it was a reproach to him that I had to do it at all"—because as head of the household he should have earned enough money for a servant. Despite their apparent community of interests, Margaret and Reo are still cultures and worlds apart.

The difference in cultures is a fact that Mead can observe scientifically as an anthropologist, though as a woman and working wife this insight does little to spare the pains. Reo carries with him the British-influenced background in which the man is dominant in most things and makes the major decisions. But she has grown up in the freer American world where the woman (above all in the Mead household) has a greater part than that and stands on an equal footing, especially intellectually. But she is attuned to the situation and Reo is not. In 1973, in *Blackberry Winter,* she writes:

> I fully realized that it was essential to respect the sensitivities of men reared in other social settings and other cultures, and that their sense of masculinity could be impaired by being asked to behave in ways they had been taught to regard as feminine. I also had a great respect for temperament, and I was resigned to having my friends display varying degrees of neuroticism which I felt was compensated for by their unusual gifts.
>
> But I thought then—as I do now—that if we are to have a world in which women work beside men, a world in which both men and women can contribute their best, women must learn to give up pandering to male sensitivities, something at which they succeeded so well as long as it was a woman's primary role, as a wife, to keep her family intact or, as a mistress, to comfort her lover. Because of their age-long training in human relations— for that is what feminine intuition really is—women have a special contribution to make to any group enterprise, and I feel it is up to them to contribute the kinds

of awareness that relatively few men—except, for example, child analysts or men who have been intimately reared by women—have incorporated through their education. And so, when Reo thought or spoke or wrote well, I was perhaps his most appreciative audience, but I did not applaud where I felt applause was not due; I criticized in situations in which I thought improvement was possible, and I was silent when I believed nothing could be done.

What seems sensible to Mead becomes a slight to Fortune. She suggests that he take a small but sunny room in the back of the apartment in which to write. He sees this as an effort to shut him out of the living room. She must not only put in a full day at the office but shop for food, cook and clean. When she returns home every evening, her arms full of bundles, to find the living room covered with Reo's papers day after day, "and without a place to rest the eye," it is, she says, "one more penalty for being a female than I could bear."

To increase the tension, *Coming of Age in Samoa* is now earning considerable royalties. Reo, deeply involved in his *Sorcerers of Dobu* (the book does not appear until 1932), has yet to see anything published. Mead puts her money safely in a small-town bank in Doylestown, Pennsylvania, while Reo loses his in a New York bank that fails.

The depression gets worse. Breadlines are everywhere, the land is blowing away (it is the time of the Dust Bowl), dispossessing farmers—the Okies wander about the southwest in search of new land—and there is much social unrest everywhere. Mead's father, basing his predictions on the falling price of gold, in the past an infallible guide, states that within ten years a world war will break out.

The tensions at home are broken by an unexpected field

trip. In the spring of 1930 they are offered the opportunity
to make a short expedition within the United States to study
an Indian culture. The Museum will give Mead $750—a piti-
fully small grant—if she will study American Indian women:
Men in all the Indian tribes from the Pacific to the Atlantic
have been thoroughly researched, but women have been ignored.

Mead is not interested.

Ruth Benedict says that if she and Reo will agree to go to
Nebraska to visit the Omaha reservation, where the remnants
of a once-great tribe are languishing in poverty and illness,
Columbia will give him a grant as well.

Nervously, in a Ford car, Margaret and Reo set out across
the country. She will study the changing role of the Indian
reservation woman; he will try to determine the role of tribal
lore in the visions young Indians are expected to experience.
It is a subject about which some broad generalizations have
been made by other investigators. In general, anthropologists
have assumed, not realizing the Omaha do not fit the pattern,
that every Plains Indian male is free to seek a vision and claim
the power it gives him; this vision gives the man his full
standing in the tribe and is his right. But this practice is not
actually followed by the Omaha. From the start Reo feels that
he is expected to confirm assumptions by no means proved,
and that if he finds otherwise he will be considered a failure.
He is certain that American scholars, interested in nothing
but their own "primitive" peoples, force their research to fit
preconceived theories and will not accept variant results.

With this psychological block hanging over him, Reo, with
Margaret, arrives at the Omaha reservation.

Heat, frightful heat.

They settle down in a frame house. The nights are so hot
they can barely get to sleep before two in the morning.

Mead hires an Indian girl as a servant; the girl is from one of the more traditional families. It is an unusual situation, for such girls do not ordinarily work as servants, but, because Mead is considered by the girl's parents to be a kind of chaperone and is trusted, she is able to gain valuable insights into Indian family life and to make friends with Indian women of various backgrounds, who serve as informants, and give her much information in the way of gossip and chatter.

Margaret has an easier time of it than Reo, who works with the men. Writing to Ruth Benedict at home, she explains the situation.

> This is a very discouraging job, ethnologically speaking. You find a man whose father or uncle had a vision. You go see him four times, driving eight or ten miles with an interpreter. The first time he isn't home, the second time he's drunk, the next time his wife's sick, and the fourth time, on the advice of the interpreter, you start the interview with a $5 bill, for which he offers thanks to Wakanda, prays Wakanda to give *him* a long life, and proceeds to lie steadily for four hours.

And, she adds, "There is a belief that death follows divulging sacred things."

Other problems Margaret and Reo face are even more discouraging. The reservation is demoralized. Once one of the great tribes of the Mississippi valley, the Omaha, a branch of the southern Sioux, have seen their lands shrink to a fraction of their former size, their hunting grounds taken by whites, the wild creatures of the forest—their food—destroyed by the advance of the settlers, their tribal structures crushed. The Omaha are in a despondent state. Their religion, once centered on visions, has become pessimistic, focused on illness and death. It is, Reo notes, a society in a "deep, very real, emotional maelstrom," due to the impact of

white influence. "Feeling and thinking are still curiously of
the old [tribal] quality, and action only has suffered a very
considerable transmutation from the influence of White contact." The Omaha, he says, show "distinctly as dissociated
personalities"—in effect their personalities were being split
between two unrelated, contradictory cultures, their minds
and emotions moulded by their own culture, while "their
hands and feet are compelled to . . . keep their bodies [free]
from hunger and privation not exactly moulded, but hewn
and battered into some apology of shape by a radically differing culture."

Broken homes, neglected children and general social disorganization are evident everywhere; Mead adds: "Drunkenness was rife."

Beside the conflict of cultural forces, the tribe is traditionally formed of two distinct sections, the members of secret
societies and those who are not members. The societies include the Buffalo, the Ghost, the Grizzly Bear, the Rattle-
snake, the Water Monster, and the Midewiwin. Also there are
the Thunder Bird, and Night Blessed or Potlatch societies.

The most powerful men in the tribe are those known as
doctors, who are especially feared by other Omaha. Doctors
possess a quality called batho^n, which is translated as "odor,"
a form of influence. Batho^n could be called good or bad: It
might cause disease, or it might cure it. In general, one stays
upwind from a doctor because one might be affected by his
batho^n.

The doctors practice shamanistic tricks to prove their
power and prestige. The uninitiated regard the tricks as mi-
raculous. Still, there is a strong element of belief even among
the doctors. Each doctor carries hidden in his clothing a sacred amulet, called an "arrow," which is seen in the form of
its symbol or representative, a terrapin, worm, lizard, snake
or insect. The arrow is passed from one generation to another.

Without the arrow the doctor dies; to dispose of it is to commit suicide.

Reo, in his graphic but twisted sentences, gives a clear instance of both the power of the arrow, and of the tragedy of drunkenness, when he describes how a drunken medicine man takes his arrow—the symbol of his secret powers, of his very life forces—from its place of concealment.

> The Omaha, when sober, often regard a drunken Omaha with an evident feeling of sheer physical repulsion almost akin to horror; quite evidently a more vivid feeling than I have, as I found when I put a drunken Indian beside sober Indians in the back seat of a car. At no time is this generalised horror raised to a greater height than where a rolling drunk leader of the Water Monster Society does what his companions regard as a possibly suicidal action. I never saw it, as it is very rare, but I heard two or three stories told me by initiates, of a leading doctor's taking his sacred arrow from his body when he was dead drunk; and the feeling about the sight of the action was still evident.

The work is more difficult for Reo than for Margaret, who gathers a great amount of material—gossip is the way in which it comes out—from the women. Reo must struggle for his material.

> The actual facts are not easily drawn from any Omaha. A similar difficulty is encountered if one attempts to discover whether an Omaha ever obtains a subsequent return present for any gift that he gives away. He does very often, far more often than not. But no Omaha will admit the bare possibility, except perhaps under the rack. Fortunately for my work on

the secret societies I had some informants literally under the rack of extreme privation and want, so I was able to penetrate into secrets that are not usually admitted.

Obtaining information under pressure from men who are on the edge of starvation may not seem a fair way of following one's profession, but Reo can show that among the Omaha, in contrast to other tribes—as far as what is known or surmised about them at any rate—membership in the secret religious societies stems from hereditary right only, membership being passed down from one generation to another, from father to son, uncle to nephew, even from grandmother to grandson. The solitary vision alone can not lead to membership. Only those with hereditary privileges can profit by a vision, normally encountered while a youth, under specific, trying, isolated conditions. The man outside secret societal structures, no matter how great his vision, can never participate in the societies. Nonmembers who claim visions were told they were liars. This discovery, so important in the comprehension of a vanishing style of life, is to be ignored by Reo's colleagues.

The task is finished at last. Work that should have taken years, perhaps even a lifetime, has been skimped into three frantic months. Both Margaret and Reo feel a sense of failure, though they have done outstanding work within the allotted time. Each will do a book about the work. Mead's is entitled *The Changing Culture of an Indian Tribe*, Reo's is called *Omaha Secret Societies*. Without the precedent of Samoa and New Guinea towering over her other work, Mead's book about Indian women would, alone, have helped make her career; now, overshadowed by her better Samoan and Manus works, it is virtually ignored.

Because of their distinctive personalities and their individual methods of working and of viewing the subject, the anthropologists' books seem like reports of two separate, unrelated tribes. Reo speaks specifically about the Omaha, and gives a clear portrayal of a society with definite characteristics. Mead calls them the Antler tribe, and, as she often does, also disguises the names and some of the case histories; her "Antler" women seem to be floating in space: They could be Mohawks or Navaho, or, as one critic remarked, even suburban white housewives.

Reo's book, *Omaha Secret Societies,* brooding, wry, joking, apologetic, by a mind that seems at home in its field but alienated in its career, is one of those oddities one might encounter in any discipline, a work so strange, moving and unusual that it cannot be categorized, and thus is set aside by the more formalistic members of the field. "I have not been excessively tender in my handling of the previous authorities," Reo remarks of the anthropological establishment, and they take the same attitude toward him. Mead can add sadly, to the account of his troubles, "This situation was so unusual, as Ruth [Benedict] had sensed, that Reo's analysis did go unrewarded. Americanists did not appreciate the detective skill, developed in his work with the Melanesian sorcerers, with which Reo had unraveled an unfamiliar fabric. . . . He is given very little [credit] for *Omaha Secret Societies,* the book in which he published the work he had the greatest difficulty in doing."

Omaha Secret Societies appears in 1932—both Reo and Margaret were again in New Guinea at the time—and the same year sees the publication of his *Sorcerers of Dobu.* Again, he does not make concessions to the public, whether the ordinary reader or the academic. His works are difficult to read at times, and express complicated theories that challenge established conceptions, or misconceptions. As with the Omaha Indians, Reo has worked

with a people who do not fit the accepted anthropological
patterns, and the experts are puzzled. The Dobuan forms
of magic are different from those of other tribes. Their
family structure, their gardens (which are planted with the
aid of magic, and prosper by magic, or falter from black
magic practiced by enemies), their kinship system, nomen-
clature, cross-cousin relationships (a favorite subject among
anthropologists, who like to know who is considered a
member of the complex clan structures and who is an outsider)—virtually everything is at variance with what others
have found or assumed.

So *Sorcerers of Dobu* is famous but unread, and even ignored. The public finds its subject interesting on the surface—for magic and sorcery are popular topics—but difficult
to understand because of the depth of its anthropological
research; the professionals find that it goes against the grain
of accepted knowledge about primitive peoples, and the reviewers either are puzzled or take a neutral stand. Only Ruth
Benedict can be overwhelmingly positive about it. Her review points out that though *Sorcerers of Dobu* is "no travel
book . . . for strangeness and intimacy, it surpasses any travel
book." And she confirms that it is "a piece of serious ethnological research." In England, the London *Times* finds it "a very
clever piece of work," and J.H. Driberg, in the *Spectator*, calls
the narrative "lucid, nervous and dramatic," believing it
should have a wider audience than mere academics. A former
teacher of Reo's, A.C. Haddon, praises the book but is curiously unable to explain its merits, which seem to be beyond
him. The anthropologist Hortense Powdermaker tempers
her review by pointing out how short a time Reo was with the
Dobu.

After the praise heaped upon his wife's books, Reo must
feel like a real second fiddle.

There is a minor consolation, if Reo ever enjoys such ironies: Despite his wife's determination to remain "Miss Mead," the reviewers, the journals and the cataloguers of his books list her as "Mrs. Reo F. Fortune."

Small reward.

Whether Miss Mead or Mrs. Fortune, Mead has long been aware that she probably cannot have children. The doctors have told her on several occasions that she has a tipped uterus, and conceiving and bearing a child is not likely, yet she can continually hope for one. However, she should plan her life differently from what it would be if she were a mother, or might easily become one. Her youthful fantasy of being the mother of six in the Reverend Cressman's drafty rectory had long ago vanished. Nevertheless her initial reluctance to marry Reo Fortune came, she says in *Blackberry Winter*, because she thought that he would "not make the kind of a father I wanted for my children," and again, "I did not think Reo . . . would make an ideal father"—if she should ever conceive. Her reason was, simply, "He was too demanding and jealous of my attention." But now she suspects that her future life with Reo will be only one of shared fieldwork and intellectual collaboration.

Her long preoccupation with the human personality and the effects a culture has upon its development is to be her primary subject. She wants to concentrate on the ways in which cultures pattern the behavior of males and females. If a boy and a girl develop different personalities by maturity, she wonders, is it because of their cultural background, or because of their biological differences, or both? Are there broad universal norms that apply to all males, to all females? These interesting and important questions have not yet been fully investigated. Mead wants to develop data in the field upon which basic theories may be projected. But where can the work be done?

Margaret and Reo consider the Navaho as a field subject, for unlike the Omaha, their culture is still alive and intact and not destroyed by the disappearance of hunting grounds. But the Navaho "belong" to Gladys Reichard and Pliny Goddard. One does not intrude upon another anthropologist's subject, no matter how great the temptation. It is a question of professional courtesy. How Reichard's and Goddard's Navaho feel is an unasked question: They probably do not know that they are "owned." So Margaret and Reo must abandon the idea of working among the Navaho, though she complains that she can do better work among them than her colleagues can.

With the Navaho ruled out, Margaret and Reo turn to an area in which they have already had some experience. It is New Guinea, with its hundreds of small and widely differing societies. Financed by royalties from *Coming of Age in Samoa* and grants from both Columbia and the American Museum of Natural History, they will study somewhere on the main island of New Guinea.

They narrow down their choice to a people known as the Arapesh who live on the New Guinea plains, about a two days' walk inland from the northeast coast of the island. The term Arapesh is the tribe's own name for human being.

In the late fall of 1931, Mead and her husband go by ship through the Panama Canal and across to New Zealand, and then to Sydney, and on to New Guinea. After a series of small, difficult journeys from one small port in New Guinea to another, they go partly up the Sepik, the main river in the area, and one on which dozens of different tribes are located. While Mead stays with a local planter, Reo goes inland to scout about and to try to round up carriers for their tons of supplies, for now, instead of the suitcase with the five dresses, the Kodak, the typewriter and the notebooks of her first trip, Mead (and Reo) will work on such a grand scale that 250 carriers are needed.

The local people have enough trade goods—knives, blankets, kettles—and are difficult to persuade to work. "They don't like carrying," she notes. She writes home, about her husband's first efforts to get porters, "Reo was pretty hopeless at first." However, Reo has his own methods of getting unruly natives to do what they do not want to do. "He went about from one village to another, unearthed their darkest secrets which they wished kept from the government, and then ordered them to come and carry."

Eventually the necessary 250 carriers are found and bullied. It requires three days to get the supplies and equipment from the tiny port town of Wewak on the coast to the plantation where Mead is resting, and two more days to carry everything from there halfway up the mountain to a hamlet called Alitoa, the site of a small, rather dreary tribe Mead labels the Mountain Arapesh, for want of a better name. The people on the coast, also an Arapesh tribe, had been noted as a gay, sophisticated group, the source of trade items and gadgets as well as of information. The Plains Arapesh are famed for a high material culture and their practice of sorcery, which makes them much feared. The Mountain Arapesh, however, are a much despised group and live in fear of the sorcerers on the plains above.

Having brought the supplies halfway up the mountainside, Reo returns for his wife, who, having sprained an ankle, must be carried in a litter along difficult, rain-soaked trails. Mead arrives safely at Alitoa. Now trouble strikes. The bearers refuse to go farther, fearing the sorcerers above, and run away. Men from other mountain tribes will not carry either. Margaret and Reo can neither continue to the plains, nor can they return to the coast. It is a desperate situation. The only choice is to make the most of it. They will work among the Mountain Arapesh, a group, Reo says, who "haven't any culture worth speaking of." He soon adds to this negative view by saying that the Moun-

An Arapesh plains sorcerer. The plains sorcerers blackmail Arapesh on the mountainsides and the coast with threats of death by sorcery (a very real threat in primitive New Guinea, where people can die for inexplicable reasons), demanding pigs, knives, rings, axes, and other trade goods. A sorcerer will not wash when practicing his magic.

tain Arapesh—the people and the culture alike—are "form-less, unattractive and thoroughly uncongenial."

They live in a native house for a week while the Arapesh build them one of their own, a huge building with a central room, bedroom, storage room, wide verandah and separate cookhouse. Reo had promised the Arapesh that they would have all the matches and salt they wanted. (Salt is the chief form of currency.) The house has cost the equivalent of $10 and is run by six young boys, called "monkeys," who do all the jobs; one of them is the shoot-boy, whose main task is to keep the kitchen supplied with pigeons.

The language is difficult to learn; the Arapesh are dispirited and have a habit of disappearing from the village, so there are long hours with nothing to do, and few ceremonies to observe and record. The culture, Mead remarks, "taxed all my now well-developed field skills to make anything of it." Unlike the relaxed life of the Coastal Arapesh, with their sixty-foot-long houses, their well-tended gardens and their extensive fishing grounds in the swamps, the Mountain Arapesh live precari-ously: Their houses are but huts, the clusters of people small, the land barren; the tribe must fish in streams. Their gardens hug the mountainsides, and this year the yam crop, one of the chief staples, is smaller than usual; the pigs, a basis of food and wealth alike, are mean and savage. The people are aware of their inferiority to the other Arapesh, and rely on them for crafts and arts. They are overseen by certain spirits, the *mar-salais*, spirits of rain, living in sanctified spots in the company of the ghosts of the dead.

Reo is driven to fury by the Arapesh, and on several occa-sions Mead must prevent him from striking one of them. Her relationship with Reo, she remarks, is again "tempestuous." But she is able to make her notes and to observe cultural differences between men and women. Yet in the end she has to conclude, "Among the Arapesh there was so little difference in the culturally expected character of men and women that I felt nothing new had been discovered." The rough edges of the culture have been rounded off—it has "soft, uncertain outlines."

However, the Arapesh do exhibit one very unusual cultural variation. An aggressor in the Arapesh culture, unlike an aggressor in virtually all other cultures, is not punished but rather his victim is blamed for having moved him to anger and violence. Unlike many primitive and advanced societies, Arapesh society does not approve of aggressive behavior in whatever form. The small, ineffectual Arapesh group is concerned primarily with the harmonious growth of living things, whether human or plant. Men are as wholly committed to this cherishing adventure as are women. She writes of the Arapesh aim for the good growth of children and of the food upon which they depend, "It may be said that the rôle of men, like the rôle of women, is maternal."

Getting even the basic material is difficult work. Mead and her husband must share a single, knowledgeable informant. When they question the people, the Arapesh complain they get headaches from having to concentrate for more than ten minutes. Still, the work is more valuable than she believes at the time.

Frustrations pile up. "I felt somehow finished," she says. She falls into a depression. Reo is away much of the time on visits to other villages. She sits alone, in this strange hamlet where the men and women fear that each generation will be progressively smaller until there are no more Arapesh, and looks out from the mountainside. The mists hide the view, and she can see only a few great leaves of pawpaw trees in the engulfing clouds. "I felt that everything ahead looked pallid and uninviting." And: "I was thirty."

The depression vanishes. Carriers are found, and they descend to the coast, to spend six weeks in recuperation. While they rest, they recall a report in *Oceania* by Gregory Bateson about the Iatmul, a tribe on the Sepik River. The Iatmul seem exciting, creative, alive. A challenge. Margaret and Reo decide that the Sepik will be the next area for study, where Bateson is now on his third trip among the Iatmul.

Immediately they have second thoughts. Much as they would like to study the Iatmul, Bateson "owns" them: They are "his." "In those days the ethics of field work were very strict," Mead laments. Another tribe must be chosen, and so they turn to the Mundugumor, neighbors of the Iatmul but culturally different.

Like the Mountain Arapesh, the Mundugumor prove to be a "disappointing choice." They are fierce cannibals who live on the high ground of a tributary of the Sepik. They have recently been put down—crushed—by the Australian administration; their ties with the past having been destroyed, the Mundugumor are now in a kind of cultural paralysis. Ceremonial life, one of the central objects of ethnological study, has ended.

The mosquitoes are frightful. In fact, mosquitoes are a constant theme in Mundugumor legend and myth, knowledge easy to enjoy at a distance but impossible to endure in the flesh. Hard and unrewarding work is Mead's verdict about this cruel, harsh people, who themselves know that their culture has been lost.

She soon loathes the tribe, for its people have endless numbers of aggressive rivalries. There is no warmth among the Mundugumor. The preferred cultural type, whether male or female, is not a warm and cherishing person but a fiercely possessive individual. Children are exploited and rejected. Unwanted babies are thrown into the river. Anger and aggressive acts are the standard, and suicide is common, often taking an odd form: A person bent on self-destruction would

get into a temper tantrum and drift downriver in a canoe, to
be captured and eaten by another tribe.

"I felt completely stalemated," she writes. To make matters worse, her tempestuous relationship with Reo takes a bad
turn professionally. In his work on the kinship system—a
basic part of anthropological research—Reo "had missed a
clue." Mead points out her husband's error. It is a tense situation. She can now equate Reo to the Mundugumor. "They
struck some note in him that was thoroughly alien to me, and
working with them emphasized aspects of his personality
with which I could not empathize."

She complains of her husband's harsh treatment of her
during illnesses. She has had many bouts of fever. He has
treated his own fevers by climbing a mountain to force the
illness out of his system. "He turned on me the same fierce-
ness with which he treated his own fevers." She gets no sym-
pathy due to his unrelenting attitudes.

"A very unpleasant three months" is her summing up.
They finish their work shortly before Christmastime, 1932. A
government launch picks them up and they chug down-
stream along the Yuat to the swift-flowing Sepik, where they
go upriver toward the government station at Ambunti where
they will celebrate the holiday. The Iatmul, Mead soon notes,
as she and Reo pass by the magnificent villages with their
great dwelling houses decorated with rattan faces woven into
the gables and the immense double-peaked men's houses in
the central plazas, are "a culture we would have liked to
study." On the way they are to pass Kankanamun, one of the
Iatmul villages where Bateson is working. The chance meeting with the rangy young Englishman will affect her as much
as any of the chance visits to remote villages in her fieldwork.

The Bateson Era

GREGORY BATESON HAS BEEN WORKING in New Guinea since 1927; in 1929 he had made a brief visit to the Sepik River area and become interested in the Iatmul, one of the more outstanding tribes; the following year he returned to spend six months at a major Iatmul village called Mindimbit, where he studied a ceremonial custom called *naven.* The naven ceremony is performed by kinsmen to celebrate various accomplishments of a child. The child—usually male, and usually initiated in groups—may be very young; there is much cruelty involved—scarring the skin with knives, and forcing the drinking of putrid water, and so on, along with attempts to frighten the subject with ghostly sounds and strange noises at night or in the depths of the initiation house. Though the rites can be performed in several ways, the principal form usually involves transvestism, the men dressing as women and the women as men. Bateson sees naven as the core of Iatmul life, and he has returned to the Sepik in 1932, to continue his work at one of the largest of Iatmul villages, Kankananum, about two hundred miles from the seacoast.

Bateson is living in a ramshackle house, in which, despite the mosquitoes and other predatory insects, he has left an opening in the roof for his cat and for a tree. It has been a

117

lonely and depressing time for him. He is not sure of his work. Many of his observations are quite tentative, for he is aware that he cannot see everything among these active, creative, aggressive people. He is not certain that basing an interpretation of Iatmul society on naven is correct. He is to say: "My field work was scrappy and disconnected—perhaps more so than other anthropologists'." He believes his work is hampered not by a lack of training but by "an excess of skepticism."

The Iatmul, one of the most powerful tribes of the Sepik, are warriors and artists. The naven ceremony is an important stage in an individual's attaining maturity. A major example of the kind of event that leads to a naven celebration is a killing, or helping others in a killing. No man is respected unless he has killed someone—a woman is as satisfactory a victim as another man. Lesser examples worthy of naven are the slaying of a crocodile or a wild pig, spearing a giant eel, even killing a small animal, or planting yams, tobacco, taro, and so on, or making certain objects, like spear-throwers or digging sticks. Naven, Bateson learns, is not only a serious rite in a person's life but it can also offer comic relief in satire and jokes, the mocking of ritual acts or of sexual intercourse. Whatever happens is due to sorcery, and much takes place under the shadow of an intangible factor called *ngglambi*, which Bateson explains as follows:

> It is thought of as a dark cloud which envelops a man's house when he has committed some outrage. This cloud can be seen by certain specialists who, when they are consulted as to the cause of some illness or disaster, rub their eyes with the white undersides of the leaves of a tree, and are then able to see the dark cloud hovering over the house of the person whose guilt is responsible for the sickness. Other specialists are able to smell

ngglambi and say that it has a "smell of death—like a dead snake."

But at the same time the Iatmul, when it suits them, can take a lighter view of sorcery, even though it causes death, for they do not share the almost paranoid view of it so characteristic of many primitive peoples, such as the Dobuans or the Mountain Arapesh.

Bateson's grand opus dealing with the Iatmul (published in 1936) shows his worrisome approach by its title. It is called *Naven: A Survey of the Problems Suggested by a Composite Picture of a New Guinea Tribe Drawn from Three Points of View*, as if he could not surmount the material he had uncovered but had to "survey" it without coming to grips with its meaning and implications. He assembles all sorts of odd facts, trying to fit them into a grand jigsaw puzzle of what naven signifies.

His reference to the significance of the nose among the Iatmul illustrates his predicament. He is attracted by the emphasis placed upon this otherwise minor characteristic. The long nose is especially admired; it is a sign of beauty in both men and women. The discovery of the nose emerges slowly, for in his tentativeness in probing the ways of the Iatmul, Bateson is not sure of its importance. "When an informant told me that Woli-ndambwi had a big nose, I wrote his statement down, but with no idea that this detail of the culture might be of any particular interest."

As artists as well as warriors, the Iatmul are famous for their ceremonial houses, some as long as 120 feet. "Magnificent buildings," remarks Bateson. The houses resemble churches superficially, but there is no true parallel, because

Where we think of a church as sacred and cool, they think of a ceremonial house as "hot", imbued with heat

by the violence and killing which were necessary for its
building and consecration.

"Hot" is the general characteristic of Bateson's Iatmul as
for Reo's Dobuans.

[In the initiation ceremonies] a boy is disciplined so that
he may be able to wield authority, so on the Sepik he is
subjected to irresponsible bullying and ignominy so that
he becomes what we should describe as an over-com-
pensating, harsh man—whom the natives describe as a
"hot" man.

The Iatmul fall into two general personality types, according to sex: the harsh, egocentric, bullying males, tense in
virtually all situations, and the lighthearted, relaxed and self-
confident women, who, though subservient to the more powerful men, are still fully developed individuals, leading lives
of psychic joys and pleasures the men resent. Often the men
are fearful in dealing with the women, for the women will
mock them when the men have made a mistake in a chant
or a ritual. The children, whether boys or girls, are brought
up alike by the women, without any special attention to their
sexual differences, until at puberty the males are taken into
the ceremonial houses for initiation. The men seem like out-
siders, visiting their wives a little uneasily, waiting for the
chance to bring their sons into the men's houses for the blood-
filled rites which mark the passage from childhood into man-
hood.

The launch bearing Margaret and Reo to Ambunti stops
at Kankananum, where Bateson is working. They go
ashore, happy to have the opportunity of meeting Bateson, about whom they have heard so much. Bateson is tall,

lank and wan, and towers well over a foot above Mead.

"You're tired," says Bateson to her. "The first cherishing words I had heard from anyone in all the Mundugumor months," she comments. She feels that she has been released from prison, a feeling that must be shared by the others, for during the past year, none of the anthropologists has met other persons with whom to discuss the work in which each has been engaged. The three of them talk all day and most of the time during the days that follow. They go to another village upstream, Ambunti, to celebrate Christmas with a group of government agents and traders, who are engaged in a continual, very drunken party. Mead makes an ethnologist's observation of the Australians: They prefer beer to champagne, and drink the latter only when the beer runs out.

Mead is becoming aware that she is drawn to Bateson, and that Reo is being left out of conversations. "By then Gregory and I had already established a kind of communication in which Reo did not share." She further defines the alienation Reo was undergoing by stating "it was always hard for him to cope with rivalry at any level."

The trio discuss future work. Bateson takes Margaret and Reo up a tributary of the Sepik, through blackwater canals dank with decaying vegetation, to Lake Tchambuli (now called Chambri). The lake is smooth as glass, with purple lotus, and pink and white water lilies, which the village women entwine in their armbands. Osprey and blue heron skim the waters. An idyllic scene. Margaret and Reo decide they will work in a village of people called, like the lake, Tchambuli, while Bateson works on the opposite shore with another group related to the Iatmul.

The Tchambuli number only 600 people; they had fled the area to escape the Iatmul, but now that the Australians have established peace, they have returned to the lake. They are more interested in art than in warfare, so their head-hunting

victims are either bought or are criminals from nearby ham-
lets. Most of the victims are criminals who have stolen food,
or infants and young children purchased from other tribes.
The Tchambuli consider it necessary that every young boy
kill someone; the boy's spear hand is guided by his mother's
brother in this first bloodletting. The victims' skulls are covered with clay and painted and hung in the men's houses. But
such head-hunting is sinking into a secondary role among the
Tchambuli. With warfare ended, they are more interested in
developing their artistic talents, and Tchambuli life is undergoing a renaissance.

Bateson comes regularly from across the lake to visit Mead
and Fortune, or they send messages back and forth. They
have endless discussions about what they are finding. Mead
is uncovering material among the Tchambuli that, fitted in
with what she has learned among the Arapesh and Mundugumor, makes a pattern. She is developing theories that she will
express in one of her most complex works, *Sex and Temperament in Three Primitive Societies.*

The three anthropologists spend endless hours in an eight-
foot-square mosquito-proof room discussing, analyzing, arguing. Each one has made important theoretical discoveries,
Mead in the realm of sexual temperaments, Fortune in kinship systems (which he will state in an article entitled "A Note
on Cross-Cousin Marriage," a work which, like his other
works, receives little recognition), and Bateson on the emotional "tone" or quality of a society.

Mead sees that among the Tchambuli the differences between men and women are markedly reversed according to
Western standards. Here the women, brisk, unadorned,
managing and industrious, fish, garden and trade. The men
are the artists and, decorated and adorned, spend their lives
in dancing, carving and painting. War is no longer a sport and
they fulfill their ritualized head-hunting with what seems like

reluctance. If men are the moody, creative, artistic individuals, a woman is measured by how well she performs her "masculine" role; if a birth is difficult for a woman, it is because she has not worked hard enough.

The theories that the anthropologists have been working out among primitive societies now seem to apply also to themselves. Here are three people from English-speaking cultures—American, New Zealand and British. It occurs to Mead that what she had posited about primitive cultures might also apply to the three foreigners.

> What if human beings, innately different at birth, could be shown to fit into systematically defined temperamental types, and what if there are male and female versions of each of these temperamental types?

She suspects that she and Bateson are the same types, that Reo is the outsider. She begins to question the traditional suppositions about male-female relationships. And she wonders if the expectations about male-female differences so characteristic of European-American cultures, the men aggressive and domineering, the women passive and "feminine," may not be reversed in societies like those of the Tchambuli, where

> women were brisk and cooperative, whereas men were responsive, subject to the choices of women, and characterized by the kinds of cattiness, jealousy, and moodiness that feminists had claimed were the outcome of women's subservient and dependent role?

Looking about the mosquito-room, she sees that "Gregory and I were close together in temperament—represented, in fact, a male and female version of a temperamental type that was in strong contrast with the one represented by Reo." She quickly adds that it would make no sense to define the traits she and Bateson shared as "feminine," any more than it would to call the behavior of Arapesh men "maternal" for being as nurturing and loving to children as the women.

But theory is one thing. Something deeper, more radical, is taking place. A marriage has now become a triangle. "Gregory and I were falling in love." They try to keep the relationship on a professional level. Coolness is the key word.

Eighteen months of work among primitive peoples are finished. It is now early 1933. Off they go, not together but following different paths. What Fortune has been thinking all along is something we can only guess at. Mead returns to the American Museum of Natural History to resume her job; she now has the apartment on 102nd Street alone. Bateson takes a freighter to England, and again assumes his post at Cambridge ("It was many weeks before I heard from him," Mead remarks). Fortune returns to New Zealand briefly, again meeting Eileen, the girl with whom he had once been so passionately in love, and then goes on to England.

Much work lies ahead for all of them, for they have not only manuscripts—articles and books—to work on but personal relations to solve. Mead finishes *Sex and Temperament in Three Primitive Societies,* Fortune some articles about the Arapesh, and Bateson his famous *Naven.* In the spring of 1935 Bateson visits the United States, where he and Mead, working with A.R. Radcliffe-Brown, tackle the problem of society, culture and character. No conclusions are reached.

By now Mead and Fortune are quietly separated, and he leaves England to go to China to teach. A marriage that had started out with high emotion, amid controversy, is ending on a subdued note. Mead's relationships with her various husbands (she will have three in all) seem to exist, to some outsid-

Lanky Gregory Bateson and Margaret Mead, newly married, discuss their work among the Iatmul at Tambunam in the Sepik River area of New Guinea. Mead wears pajamas under her skirts as protection against the overwhelming and ferocious New Guinea mosquitoes.

ers, in a kind of unreal world; the men are not listed in the various "official" biographies or fact sheets about her, and one wonders if they may not be merely some kind of drone to her worker bee.

Mead works out another faraway rendezvous, this time with Bateson. They will meet in Java, the principal island of the Dutch East Indies, marry there, and then go to neighboring Bali for an immense project that will consume several years of their time. But upon arriving in Java they find that complications prevent their marrying. They must fly over to Singapore for the ceremony.

Bateson is thirty-one, Mead thirty-four. She remarks that both look younger than they are. He is more than a head taller than she. Photographs of them look like two unrelated pictures in different scales pasted together into a composite. Mead can remark that she grew up at eleven, while Gregory still looked "asthenic"—slightly built—and that his silhouette was adolescent.

They go by ship back to the East Indies, first to Java and then to Bali. By now it is March 1936.

The Balinese are a sharp contrast to Mead's other cultures. In Bali, instead of a handful of Stone Age people, she and Bateson are to study one of the most complex of all the nontechnological societies, one she can equate in many aspects to medieval Europe.

Balinese society is both feudal and communal. Even the most ordinary act in daily life may bear a religious significance. The Balinese follow a diluted, relaxed form of Hinduism, with traces of Buddhism, the result of religious, economic and cultural colonization by Indians some ten to twelve centuries earlier. The rulers are descendants of the Indian *kshatriya* or warrior caste (in Bali known as *kasatria*), who dominate a Brahmin priesthood and a large number of now-casteless people.

Bali is to present a new height in fieldwork for Mead, and new challenges. The Balinese culture has a dreamlike character, and indeed trances, divination and numerous rites and ceremonies of esoteric origins form the core of everyday life; witches are common and are feared. The arts and crafts are highly developed, and the air is filled with music. Numerous plays entertain the people. Balinese society, already much studied, possesses written records, a long cultural history, reliable informants and much ceremony to observe and record. In Bali, Mead is no longer at the mercy of bearers afraid of sorcerers or at the whim of informants who are likely to disappear for unknown reasons.

After much discussion, she and Bateson move to a mountain village, where life is simpler than on the crowded plain. Here they have a house built for the two years they will be on the island. Mead and Bateson, who are collaborating instead of working as friendly rivals, as had been the experience with Reo, have a team of anthropologists and assistants to aid them, among them Jane Belo, who records ceremonies (Belo is particularly interested in the births of twins, to the Balinese a most unfortunate event), Colin McPhee, a musicologist, Walter Spies, who annotates music and works on the arts, and Katherine Mershon, a specialist in dance and religious behavior. There are also skilled secretaries and interpreters. And instead of the primitive equipment she had carried to Samoa—half a dozen notebooks and a folding Kodak—she and Bateson not only have the most advanced photographic equipment but even a movie camera.

Bali, Mead states, is "sheer heaven for the anthropologist."

We feasted on riches, day after day, and found each temple, each theatrical performance, and each shadow play more delightful and more intelligible than the last. . . . Bali was a high culture. . . .

But even life in the primitive mountain village, which they chose because they wanted a simple, uncomplicated society, is for an anthropologist highly complex. Bateson and Mead originally planned on taking some 2,000 photographic negatives, but will finish with 25,000. They must send home for bulk film, and improvise ways of loading cassettes. At night they develop each day's shooting. She finds she must now make ten times as many notes because of the tremendous number of photographs they are taking.

All is overwhelming in this feast of riches. They must study not one birth celebration but twenty; they watch and photograph young girls going into trances on fifteen different occasions, and must compare six hundred small carved kitchen gods from one village with five hundred from another; forty paintings a man did of his dreams are compared with the dream paintings of another hundred men. The opportunity for such work, Mead notes, is "dazzling," "so rich" is the material, and the progress in method and theory "exhilarating."

The very complexity of Balinese life inevitably results in a diffusion of her perceptions and her results. In place of the concise to-the-point focus of her work in Samoa, Manus and New Guinea, her researches among the Balinese are to serve more as a counterpoint for her analysis of men, women and children in the other societies. Her one general work is the magnificent photographic study she does with Bateson. Their *Balinese Character* is their only joint effort. It is based upon the 25,000 photographs that Bateson shoots, edited down to less than 800. (It is not published until 1942.)

Unfortunately for Mead's collaborative efforts, Bateson loses interest in this kind of study later and turns to other projects covering an amazing scope—he interviews schizo-phrenics and studies octopuses, otters and dolphins on the way to developing theories that lie outside Mead's own fields. But for her the work among the Balinese is not wasted. They form one of the seven societies in *Male and Female* (published in 1949) and get written up in technical papers she is to do upon her return from her second trip to Bali in 1939.

The two allotted years pass as if in a Balinese trance. Suddenly Mead and Bateson awaken to the fact that their work has run its course. They have completed their project. It is time to go. The war that Professor Mead had once predicted is ominously close: Hitler has occupied Austria and will soon invade Czechoslovakia. On the way back home to New York Mead and Bateson decide to spend a few months with the Iatmul to fill out some unfinished studies.

It is a difficult time. Bateson is often ill, and the Iatmul have been disrupted by an extended dry spell. Obtaining the necessary material—on the ways in which the Iatmul and the Balinese contrast in such things as raising children—requires extended work. Another six months pass.

Before they return home, they go back to Bali again in an effort to do some last-minute research before Europe's coming war prevents international travel. At home in New York again Mead and Bateson turn to their great masses of material, trying to assemble it into coherent form. And then, she writes, "The war engulfed us."

PART TWO

Immigrants and Natives

MARGARET MEAD DIVIDES HER WORLD—and all worlds—into two sections. The turning point is World War II, which ends the many thousands of years of past history and contains the seeds of all events to come, present and future. She points out that when the first atom bomb exploded at the end of World War II, only a few people understood that all mankind was entering a new age. Of those born before the war, now adults, she says, they are *all* "today immigrants in a changing world." The changing world belongs to the young generations, the people of tape recorders, atomic energy, Beatles: They share a common culture, while the adults are separated from each other by culture, language, customs, birth. The adults' world is a "foreign" world. They are strangers even in their own country. But "all children, in whatever part of the world in which they are growing up, are native to the kind of world in which they take for granted the thinking toward which their parents can only grope." Further:

In 1957, when Sputnik was launched, American and Russian children were fully able to visualize our new relationship to space as a reality; a few years later, among the Manus of the Admiralty Islands, school children expressed almost identical ideas about space exploration. The young are able to adapt because they are not burdened or confused by out-of-date information.

It is technology that has transformed the present world, and it is technology that can help now in the creation of a shared future for all the peoples of the earth. We cannot share in the past of peoples whose traditions are very different from ours, nor can others share easily in our past. But now . . . the whole world, through technology, experiences events simultaneously.

The problem for the prewar generations, Mead states—a theme she repeats often, in articles and speeches—is how to become citizens of the community—a Global Village, less and less restricted except superficially by boundaries, language and race—of which our children are the true natives.

This insight, which is so basic to her later thinking, and one which she has tried to convey to parents anxious and worried over the generation gap, is one that developed gradually. Two major events might be found to lie in the background, one the birth of her daughter, the other the unexpected emergence of the Manus as a twentieth-century people.

Mead had been told many times by doctors that she would never have children; she suffered many miscarriages with all her husbands. When she and Bateson made their brief return to Bali in 1939, she was sure she was pregnant. She was carried through the mountain roads in a bamboo chair. But one night the chair collapsed as she was being carried, and she again had a miscarriage. On the return home to New York, she was sure she was pregnant again, and this time she took even greater precautions against an accident. She cancelled a planned trip to England with Bateson, and stayed at home in the utmost quiet.

The year was a difficult one. In September Germany invaded Poland, and Great Britain and France declared war against Hitler. Bateson returned to his homeland for whatever wartime duties he might be asked to perform. Meanwhile Mead had met a young physician named Benjamin Spock, and talked to him about the problems of her pregnancy. Spock introduced her to an obstetrician, Claude Heaton, who was interested in American Indian medicine; he agreed with her that she could avoid taking an anesthetic during childbirth unless it became absolutely necessary, and that she should be allowed to nurse her baby, a practice then contrary to most medical thinking.

So Mead could prepare herself for natural childbirth, an idea that was then rare. Instead of worrying about the pains of labor, she could learn and think about the task of having the baby. "The male invention of natural childbirth has had a magnificent emancipating effect on women, who for generations had been muffled in male myths instead of learning about a carefully observed actuality," she says in *Blackberry Winter.*

But she still has apprehensions about the coming baby. What will it look like? She realizes that there were "members of my family whom I did not find attractive or endearing, and I knew that my child might take after them. Distinguished forebears were no guarantee of normality. But what I dreaded most, I think, was dullness." But she can also worry about other traits in the family tree, deafness, mongolism and one child with cerebral palsy.

On December 8, 1939, Mary Catherine Bateson is born, her birth being well photographed by a woman named Myrtle McGraw. Mead, who has spent so much time studying children in other lands, will now have the opportunity to keep extensive records in both photographs and text of her daughter's growth and development. Mead had planned on bringing up the baby in Cambridge, England, where Bateson was affiliated, but the outbreak of the war prevents that, and so she remains in New York. Although Bateson had gone home to see about his military service, after the invasion of Poland and its occupation by the Germans, the hostilities have abated, and there is very little fighting at the time, so Bateson is told to finish his work in America, and he returns to New York to his wife and baby.

"We called her Cathy," she writes. "She was fair-haired, her head was unmarred by a hard birth or the use of instruments, and her expression was already her own. I was completely happy." Mead goes to stay with her parents in Philadelphia. "Bringing up Cathy was an intellectual as well as an emotionally exciting adventure."

I believed that the early days of infancy were very important—that it made a difference how a child was born, whether it was kept close to its mother, whether it was breast-fed, and how the breast feeding was carried out.

Cathy is "an early-responsive child" and Mead—and Bateson—are at her side to record every moment, awake and asleep. The baby is probably one of the most studied children in history: Certainly few children have had so expert an anthropologist to chart their growth. From the beginning Mead takes notes, following both her family's custom and her own training, about everything relating to Catherine; notes about breast-feeding, about when she cries or smiles, when she sleeps and speaks.

While Bateson had been in England, Mead had hired a young girl from Appalachia as a nurse for the baby. But Bateson is afraid the woman, with her backcountry accent, will give Catherine bad speech habits, and so he finds an English nanny whose language he approves.

Bateson, immersed in the Bali project, cannot draw ade-

Gregory Bateson with baby Catherine. Cathy, the daughter of two of this century's most famous anthropologists, is probably one of the most photographed and most studied children ever born.

quate funds from England because of wartime currency re-
strictions, so Mead goes back to work, teaching anthropology
part-time at New York University and working part-time at
the American Museum of Natural History, and caring for the
baby during her free moments.

In December 1941, with the bombing of Pearl Harbor by
the Japanese, the United States, too, is brought into the war.
Bateson is already working in New York on a wartime project
for England, and now Ruth Benedict enlists Mead in a series
of jobs for the United States government.

The war years are an especially busy period for Mead. In
the year before America's entry she had begun a study of the
existing psychiatric literature on psychosomatic medicine, to
search for links between illnesses and social patterns. This
work is interrupted by her wartime duties. She is appointed
Executive Secretary and Director of Research of the Committee on Food Habits of the National Research Council, a
post she holds, despite many interruptions, until the end of
the war in 1945. This job entails much travelling about the
country to talk to people setting up food programs.

In 1943 she makes a trip to Britain, where many young
American GIs are preparing for the coming invasion of Ger-
man-occupied Europe, as a lecturer and "interpreter" of
American-British relations, for both governments had discovered that there were vast cultural differences between their
people.

Mead is often aided by a young anthropologist, Rhoda Métraux, a pupil of Malinowski and Benedict who joins her in
studies of American attitudes toward nutrition, rationing and
the problems of feeding Europe after the fighting ended.
Mead and Métraux will continue over the years to study
American culture together, and, at a distance, the cultures of
France, Russia, China and Germany, and eventually, collabo-
rate in fieldwork in New Guinea.

An energetic and inveterate proselytizer for her "Global Village," Margaret Mead never misses a chance to make her views known to the world. Here she addresses peoples of all races, cultures and nations on a United Nations broadcast. Mead can and does speak on virtually any topic, from the minutiae of daily living to the great problems of mankind.

Part of the time Mead and Bateson share a household with another couple, Larry and Mary Frank; the two families also vacation in New Hampshire, where they take in some refugee children from England. The war years are hectic: Mead, Bateson and Larry Frank are constantly moving about, from New York to Washington to Europe, and by the time the war ends, Bateson and Mead seem to spend more time apart than together.

By 1950 they are formally divorced, leaving Mead alone with her daughter. Bateson goes to California to begin a career of teaching and research; he accepts a post at Stanford University as Visiting Professor of Anthropology, and also teaches anthropology, cybernetics and psychiatry at the veterans' hospital at Palo Alto. Bateson, like the other husbands, seems to have played a role as a "collaborator"; he is the man who successfully impregnated her. Personal relationships are far removed. In fact, one of the reviewers of *Blackberry Winter*, Jane Howard, writing in *The New York Times*, points out that "Although none of her three marriages endured, she takes enormous pride in having finally become a mother . . . and in time a grandmother." Miss Howard adds that "What one misses most in this lucid, witty record . . . is more candor about the author's three husbands. . . . We are offered few marital vignettes of the sort that lend charm to Dr. Mead's sketches of her forebears."

Mead's constant travels bring her to Australia in 1952 on a lecture tour, and here she is told a strange story. She had been looking for new possibilities of study; her Australian colleagues convince her "that the most useful thing I could do was a restudy of Manus, where, it was reported, the most extraordinary things were going on."

The Manus, who had never expected to see Mead again— nor she them—were undergoing a series of drastic changes that, as she noted much later, took them five thousand years in half a century. When she and Reo left them, she thought they would deteriorate into one more abject version of the New Guinea work-boy, not fully native, not properly Western, but an unhappy mixture of both. Instead, on their own initiative, after exposure to both Japanese and Allied forces during World War II, they had begun to redesign their own culture, and moved as a group—grandparents, parents and children—into their own version of Western, and specifically American, culture.

What happened to the Manus was partly due to chance, partly due, at first, to events over which they had no control, and then to their own very skillful and intelligent insights into what it meant to be a member of the new world. In a sense, they were less "immigrants" from the past than "natives" of the new generation. Until the end of the war they were like a canoe smashed in a storm, they drifted with the course of history. Only when the war ended were they able to take matters into their own hands, to rescue themselves.

The change was so dramatic, so incomprehensible to the Australians who administered New Guinea and the Bismarck Archipelago, that they felt that Mead, the only person except for Reo who had thoroughly studied the Manus as a primitive culture, could understand what was happening. How, the Australians wanted to know, could she explain the strange events that had turned these seagoing ex-cannibal traders into adaptable members of the mid-twentieth century?

It is a challenging question, and she draws up a request for a grant from the Rockefeller Foundation, to be channelled through the American Museum of Natural History, for a restudy of the Manus. It is awarded to her, and she goes about making preparations for a return to Manus.

Field trips are becoming progressively more complicated, though now anthropologists can travel by plane in a day

or so instead of by a boat trip of several months. But because the scope of study expands with each trip, more and
more people are involved and the means of making the
study require more and more technology. It takes Mead
a year to plan the trip, and to find the right assistant.
She queries departments of anthropology—now a popular
subject—for "a graduate student who was well qualified in
linguistics, theoretical and applied electronics and photog-
raphy and who was interested in culture and personality
studies." Only one person fits her demanding qualifica-
tions, a young man named Ted Schwartz, whose wife,
Lenora, also wants to do fieldwork.

In June 1953 Mead and the Schwartzes fly down to the
Admiralties. She settles down in Peré, and the Schwartzes in
Bunai, some forty-five minutes away by boat, where they can
carry on independent studies but easily keep in touch with
her when necessary. This is not the Manus she and Reo had
studied, but another world entirely. And as the Australians
had said, strange events had occurred.

The Manus, Mead soon finds out, unlike so many other primitive societies, had not stood alone and isolated, slowly dying
out while the rest of the world rushed into the nuclear, electronic age. The island's slim contacts with the West had not
brought illness, death, the rupture of soul force, the end of a
simple culture, but a radical change in life. Like Cathy, the
Manus were "born" into the new world, the world of which
they, and she, are the "natives" and in which Mead, anthropologist and mother, is an "immigrant." In both the
Stone Age primitives and the tiny, attuned, intellectual
daughter one can find sources of Mead's insights into generation gaps and new societal structures. The Manus, analyzing
their own situation in the light of what they could view of the
more powerful industrial West, would escape the fate of

other peoples, not only in the South Pacific but in Asia, Africa and the Americas.

The tribe was shrewd and businesslike. The leaders understood that the religion of the West, Christianity, was a far more powerful force than their own cults of spirits and ancestral dead. They realized that if they adopted Christianity, many of their own religious customs and beliefs must perish, notably the cult of Sir Ghost, that noisy, demanding supernatural being who inhabited the households, scolding, punishing, berating people for their sexual and economic sins. There had been much discussion in Peré over what course to take, and after careful consideration, the Manus, for purely practical reasons, adopted Roman Catholicism. The Protestants had the disadvantage of collecting tithes, taught in the local languages, and did not practice confession. The Catholics did not tithe, taught the widely spoken Pidgin (otherwise formally called neo-Melanesian) and practiced the rite of confession, a rite the Manus also practiced. The Catholics had the additional advantage of secret confessions, in contrast to the public confessions the tribe enjoyed.

So the Manus threw out Sir Ghost and other spirits, and with them the amulets and charms that had been so necessary a part of their lives. They told Mead, who documented the many steps in the Manus entry into the modern world in her *New Lives for Old*, that in looking back upon the ghost cult they could feel that the spirits were like childhood fears.

The 1929 police-boy strike that had happened after Mead and Fortune passed through New Guinea had taught the Manus that the whites were not infallible or invincible. Throughout the entire New Guinea area, from the tiny offshore islands and the strings of archipelagos to the sandy shores and the remote mountains, the people were restless. Everywhere there were hints of a new world to come, a millennium, when the black peoples would replace the whites, when the foreigners would give up their ill-gotten spoils and return the land to the native people. However, except for the movement led by Paliau, the Manus police-boy who had been one of the strike leaders, little active rebellion took place until after World War II.

After his police service had been completed, Paliau returned home to Manus. Mead learned that he had come back to a culture in ferment. Various reforms were being talked about, she established, as people tried to grapple with what were evident abuses in Manus society. Attempts were being made to stop the constant bickering among people, especially that which resulted from the remnants of the ghost cults. Another police-boy attacked the traditional marriage system, which lay at the foundation of the cruel form of bondage of young men to older men who had financed their weddings. This man wanted the Manus to try a modern way of life, including "working for a living [instead of trading], buying European goods, and dressing up like Europeans." Paliau joined in the call for reform.

But events moved slowly on Manus. The war which Mead and Fortune had feared broke out, and the Admiralty Archipelago was occupied by the Japanese, who ruled with much repression and some torture to keep the people in line. It was with joy that the Manus told Mead of the American attack and counter-occupation. Allied armies, primarily American, landed in force and set up bases. One million Americans were to pass through this tiny, isolated territory with its population of 13,000; in comparison, Great Britain, with its forty million people, saw but two million American troops over a longer period.

Mead could understand the profound effect that the Americans had. For primitive tribes whose currency was shells, dogs' teeth, sometimes pigs and a few silver shillings, the effects were overwhelming. Not only did the

Americans have everything on a grand, virtually unimaginable scale, including much the Manus never dreamed existed, but they were also very generous with whatever they possessed. Americans shared food, drinks, movies, medical care, transportation with the Manus, Usiai and Mantankor. For the first time the people—and this is something that happened all over the Pacific—experienced racial equality. They also saw American black troops, though in segregated units, being treated pretty much as the white soldiers were treated.

Mead charted the Manus change of attitudes carefully. Another impressive factor for the people was that the Americans had machines to do the heavy work. Arduous physical labor, which would have required weeks, even months, for native laborers, would be quickly performed by giant machines. Jungles were cleared, airstrips leveled, garbage pits dug, all by bulldozers. Also the Americans took care of their sick with medicines that worked, instead of exposing them to the mysteries of witch doctors and incantations. More, the Americans were not at the mercy of Sir Ghost, with his mysterious penances for some economic or sexual sin inflicted in the form of illness. Illness was something the Americans treated immediately and efficiently. The Americans put the highest value on good health, and they shared their medical treatment with the Manus.

Other Pacific societies were found to have undergone somewhat similar experiences, but Mead could see in 1953 that few but the Manus were able to take a practical and positive view of events. American generosity and democracy had a profound effect upon Manus thinking, and led them to action. Under the Germans and Australians the native was an outcast in his own land; he could not enter the white man's house nor eat from his dishes nor receive his medicine. But now a Manus could enter an American's tent, join him on the chow line, sit next to him at the outdoor movies, lie in an adjoining bed in the infirmary, get equal treatment from white doctors and nurses.

Suddenly the Americans were gone, to other islands, to Japan, to their homes. The war had moved on, was over, peace ruled throughout the Pacific islands. On Manus the people were open to the return of the police-boy Paliau, and to his message of a new world, a world that would be the Manus version of what the Americans came from.

Paliau is a natural, straightforward orator, with a disarming frankness, a quality that impresses Mead. In writing home, she describes him thus:

Paliau is a man of about 45, possibly a little less, slight, pleasant, with the quiet assurance of a man who has always been able to think about what he wanted to think about and a manner which can only be described as quietly vice-regal. I have come to the conclusion that the essence of his genius is the completeness of his conception. All the people of the South Coast—and ultimately of the whole of the Admiralties—were to be welded into one unit and all the changes which would make it possible for them to belong to the modern world were to be made at once. A new kind of house, new clothes, a new calendar, a new social organization, a new form of church, a new ethic, and all the institutions necessary to support these things—a treasury, taxes, customs, a school, a hospital—all these were to be set up at once. He worked out the necessary negotiations to find space for the Manus villages on shore and supplied the design within which their entire life was rebuilt—on shore—while the Usiai (the bush people of the big island) came down to the sea coast and learned to live with the Manus and use boats.

Many people saw, as did Mead, an inner reserve which could never be broached. Paliau did not confide in others, and to the end he stood as a leader alone, ahead of and above the others. In the beginning, his message was in part mystical, based on visions, dreams and inspiration: The Garden of Eden would reappear if only sin were abolished (he was especially concerned with people's antisocial behavior such as stealing, quarreling and lying). Paliau also preached that a new world would come, the dead would rise, gifts would come to the people and they would gain their freedom from the whites. This kind of messianic expectation is known as a Cargo Cult, or Cargo movement, and Paliau's message was in the main-stream of the movement.

Cargo was a long-smouldering tradition, known through-out the world. Loosely defined, Cargo is the belief that some-day the people of this or that place (the locale is most often the South Pacific) will receive certain material goods now possessed by whites and denied black and brown peoples by white selfishness. Belief in Cargo first arose in the nineteenth century when Europeans began to appear in numbers in the Pacific, as well as in Africa and parts of Asia. Cargo-type movements were noticed among the Maori of New Zealand, the Hawaiians and the Fijians, and also among the American Indians, Siberians, Africans and Chinese (the Ghost Dance movement and the Boxer Rebellion are famous examples) where the white presence was widespread and forceful.

South Pacific Cargo received its greatest impetus during World War II, after the arrival of American troops, who appeared suddenly and without notice on dozens of islands with unlimited quantities of strange Western goods, from war materiel to washing machines, movie theaters, Nissen huts, eating utensils, canned foods, candy bars and chewing gum, beer and whiskey and other luxuries undreamed of by people scarcely out of the Stone Age. Few of the islanders had any contact in the past with whites, and they made the natural assumption that such goods were the product of magic and if the white man could make such wonders appear by magic— for there seemed to be no other explanation, the islanders having no conception of the factory and the assembly line— could not the black, brown, red and yellow man also make things appear by his own magic?

Various messiahs arose everywhere, promising both the coming of Cargo by ship or plane and an end to white domination. Few of these messiahs lasted more than a short time: Cargo did not come as promised. Followers of the messiahs lost faith, turned to other leaders, or gave up the idea of Cargo, disillusioned and bitter. Some tribes reverted to their original subservient role as colonial subjects, passive and inward-turning. Others, maturing from the experience, saw the solution in political action, or in labor organizations, cooperatives and national parties.

The Manus were among the people to go through the Cargo experience and emerge more mature and independent, thanks to Paliau's own spiritual, psychological and political development. Where many other Cargo leaders remained on the level of the medicine man or witch doctor, Paliau developed into a true leader of charismatic qualities.

Paliau's impact was so powerful that Mead found that the Manus marked his arrival as the beginning of a new era and dated their calendar on it. He began to acquire a kind of supernatural aura. But shortly he abandoned his otherworldly themes and advocated more practical courses based upon his experiences in the outside world. He now emphasized a break with the past: Throw out the costly customs that have been such a burden to us, he told the

Manus. Stop wasting money on dowries and burial feasts. Use a currency more practical than dogs' teeth. Get rid of customs whereby a woman has several husbands, or a man several wives.

Not only must the wasteful practices of the past be discarded, but the people should cooperate for a better world. The sea people and the land people must work together, must share their resources. "The most remarkable aspect of the movement," an Australian government report issued in 1950 said, was "the achievement of Paliau in getting traditionally hostile seafaring and land-dwelling Manus native population groups to work together." The Manus had learned that if they cooperated wisely with each other they would soon have enough of the white man's goods to be able to live like white men, a premise whose worth was not challenged then, though it was to be a quarter of a century later. It seemed like a sensible proposition, and the practical and energetic Manus saw the reasons behind it.

Paliau demanded effort from his followers. He saw that the good life would not come without work. He insisted on peacefulness and good neighborliness, elementary methods of hygiene and sanitary improvements, and especially better housing and schools, viewing the latter as the places where the doctrines of a new world could be taught.

Mead could see that Paliau was not doing a mere patching up here and there. His reforms went to the core of Manus life. His insights into the problems of tribal structure were broad and advanced. He noted the low position of women and called for the end of traditional marriage practices, which would not only free the women but make marriage easier for the young men who lacked the necessary wealth for the bride price. Consequently, a number of young women, moved by his ideas, ran away from their husbands. Paliau gave them shelter, bringing the charge against him in Australian newspapers (which were not particularly sympathetic to the independent attitudes of their government's wards) that he was "the harem-keeping mogul of a 'Cargo cult.'"

Two brief imprisonments of Paliau a few years before Mead's arrival did not stop the movement, and the Australians released him. The last major step Paliau took was to move Peré. He convinced the Manus that they should have a new, "modern" village, on land instead of over the edge of the lagoon. A new town was carefully planned, houses were built on a magnificent piece of land along a beach, with a central plaza as the core of the new Peré. The sweep of the plaza was soon truncated for a school, which was so popular that the children of the neighboring villages were also sent to it.

Problems arose. The step into the new world, the Manus found, was also accompanied by modern headaches. Overcrowding, pollution and juvenile delinquency came to plague the village. Still, the people, who Mead had thought would soon fade away as a tribal proletariat, subject to the conflicting forces of a faraway government, the fluctuating demands of the copra planters on other islands and the stultifying traditional social structure, were now, by their own efforts, a dynamic, progressive little nation.

The Australians' suggestion to revisit the Manus was, Mead realized, a unique and unusual opportunity, for although anthropologists sometimes returned to societies they had studied, it was primarily to reexamine aspects they had slighted previously or to search out material to refute criticism from other anthropologists. Few ever returned a full generation later to see what had happened to a culture, especially one which had experienced radical, self-sought changes for the better.

Now Mead is back after half a lifetime to learn what has happened to the children of her own youth, the children she had so carefully studied for *Growing Up in New Guinea.*

So in the new Peré she gets her own house, not on the edge of a lagoon as previously, but one on the village's new ceremonial square. She has a magnificent view of the mountains and but a two-minute walk to look at the ocean. Because open land is at a premium, the houses, ringed around the square on three sides, are close together: Her neighbors are within six feet of her, so that she can look directly from her windows into theirs—"excellent for field work," she remarks.

Mead seems more mellow, more at ease in the new Peré. "Although the houses lack the style of the old village, on the whole it seems more beautiful," she can note. And of the new Peré inspired by Paliau she writes, "The astonishing thing about all this is that it seems to work." Instead of the harsh battles of the past, when "the air used to be blue with fury," she hears not one quarrelling voice.

Modernization seems to appeal to the Manus, for they are doing it according to their own desires, not according to plans drawn up by some faraway U.N. mission or the Australian government. On the broad view, they are looking forward to a federation of all the diverse tribes of the great island, united in brotherhood and a truly modern society. Paliau had hoped to eliminate the traditional tribal jealousies, to build a kind of utopia—a perfect state—not only based upon an adaptation of European law but one which would also stress good-humored friendliness instead of feuds, supernatural curses, sorcery and unbridled anger. The ancestral spirits that still inflicted so much psychic and even physical damage upon people would be replaced with the One God. Education would replace the ancient initiatory trials that the young men were forced to undergo, and there would be an end to local warfare and head-hunting.

The world is changing rapidly, Mead realizes. Even in the West, the transformations from the prewar period to the present are immense. Europeans and Americans have been jolted from a dying feudal economy into the nuclear, electronic age, and the Manus have decided wholeheartedly to step with the West into the same world.

In 1928 the young married women, Mead remembers, were still "primitives." Their heads had been shaved to show their state; their earlobes were weighed down with ornaments of dogs' teeth and shells, and their clothing was but two small aprons, one in front, one in back, made of pandanus grass. But even then they were in the process of abandoning such traditional dress for the shapeless cloth clothing introduced by the missionaries throughout the Pacific. In 1953 Mead found the women, especially the young ones, in contemporary cotton dresses, their earlobes bare, and the use of tatoos fading away. Along with their children and grandchildren, these women had entered into the new world as a group—there was no generation gap, but the movement of an entire people into the contemporary world.

Now all the children went to school. The idea had come from a Peré man, who during the war had been given two years of schooling by an itinerant chaplain. When the people of Peré decided to modernize their village, this young man had insisted on the village's having a school. A kind of "shadow" school was built for the real school of the future. The children were sorted by size, and the young man taught them numbers and letters. Later they not only had a real schoolhouse but a real teacher from outside, an Australian.

Even the peoples' names had been Westernized. Loponiu now called himself Johanis Lokus, Kapeli was Stefan Posangat, and so on. Pokanau, one of Mead's informants in 1928, now wore a khaki shirt and shorts like those of an Australian, and because of his great knowledge of traditional ceremonies and rites, he was called the "lawyer man."

The Manus, Mead reports, were perhaps the most successful model of adjustment she had ever recorded. The people were practical, enterprising, interested in the manner in which things worked, open to taking chances with their children and confident of their own ability to cope with the new world. They were making a good adjustment to the demands of the larger system of the twentieth century.

An entire system was transformed, releasing extraordinary amounts of energy. The exploitative kinship patterns of the past, in which the young men, as well as the women, were at the mercy of their elders, and feared the illnesses caused by avenging spirits, had disappeared in favor of the group achievement, cooperative actions and pride in mastering the demanding and superior institutions of the West. "It seemed," Mead states, "that self-initiated, complete change was better and more efficient than piece-meal change in which people partly adjusted to partial change, as a man might limp on a sprained ankle, exacerbating the inflammation."

She thinks that the Manus might be a pattern for the millions of other primitive and colonial people caught between old and new worlds, and that their example might make the transition for others smoother than had been expected.

She stays with the Manus at New Peré for six months, recording the ways in which change has taken place. The Schwartzes stay another six, and then visit an expedition in New Britain before coming home. The night Mead leaves, she is given a feast, as she had been given one twenty-five years earlier. And again the Manus do not expect her to return, for everyone is getting old. Many Manus do not—or did not then, due to inadequate medical care—live long enough to see their grandchildren, and Mead is almost fifty-three. Pokanau, perhaps closer to her than any other Manus, says formally to her, "Now, like an old turtle you are going out into the sea to die, and we will never see you again." The image is one that seems to intrigue her, and both she and the Manus think that this *is* the last time they will see each other.

Her work on the Manus seems to have brought the tribe up to date. They have joined the modern world, their new lives are amply documented and whether or not she will return again is not a pressing question. She has several other jobs to engage her, and a daughter to raise. Catherine is now fifteen.

Catherine seems to be a duplicate of her mother, and of her grandmother and great-grandmother: self-sufficient, intelligent, seeing life as a system and rather aware that there was no one like Catherine. One of her classmates remembers that when they were very young Catherine always had the most interesting items to display at Show and Tell—primitive masks, flutes, drums, grass skirts and other artifacts that no other child could even dream of bringing to kindergarten. Catherine knew she was far ahead of the others.

But Catherine is only one of Mead's activities. She has proved that she can be a working mother, and work she does, with an energy and a fury that leave others behind. Articles, books, reports roll out with regularity. Her main base, her home, her cave, her Stone Age retreat, is always her niche under the Museum's eaves. When she joined the Museum in 1926 it was as an assistant curator. She has not seemed overly ambitious on the job; her successes lie outside her cave. She did not become an associate in her department until 1942, at a time when she had a handful of other things to balance: her work for the government, committees to run—whatever the war effort required—a book or two to turn out.

When the war ended—and Bateson was on his way to other fields—she began to branch out, and from here on it is hard to follow her tracks. One can see the major roads she pursued, but some of the byways disappear in the blur of her speed, and the chronology overlaps. One of her first major outside posts is at Columbia University, where she becomes Director of Research in Contemporary Cultures, and then a professor of anthropology at the university and a special lecturer there; she also takes a post at Fordham as chairman of the Social Science Department and professor of anthropology, in the late 1960's.

But these posts, which would be enough for the ordinary individual, are only a beginning. She becomes Visiting Professor in the Department of Psychiatry at the University of Cincinnati, the Sloan Professor at the Menninger Foundation, the Alumni Association Distinguished Professor at the University of Rhode Island, the Fogarty Scholar in Residence for the National Institute of Mental Health, a member of the American Anthropological Association (becoming its president in 1960), and so on, with membership in such organizations as the American Ethnological Society, the Society for Women Geographers, the World Federation for Mental Health, the World Society for Ekistics. After a while one gives up the listing and wonders how she can fill so many chairs, participate in so many conferences, within the finite time of the ordinary day.

Her books appear almost annually. Some are in collaboration with associates or former students, some are mere collections of past work, some are collections of papers by others, with her name as editor, a few are original works. But now she is becoming diffuse, verbose, repeating herself, sounding like a wise, old grandmother who knows the world all too well and wants her children to do as she says—and does (no one

With United Nations members Arthur Lewis (left) and C.V. Nara-simhan (right), Margaret Mead speaks before U.N. TV cameras on the organization's Technical Assistance Program's tenth anniversary of aid to underdeveloped nations in 1959. Mead has firm ideas of the ways in which the poorer lands are intimately linked to the richer nations, believing all nations are joined by modern communications and technology.

can complain that she has not done incredible things)—but she always speaks with authority.

Her *Rap on Race*, a dialogue with the black writer James Baldwin, seems like a book with great possibilities, but the reviewers complain that it was ill-prepared and not very deep. The two had never met before. They spent an hour getting acquainted, and then the next day, in two sessions, talked about race and society. The "book seems like an urbane conversation of a Swarthmore liberal and a literary young Philadelphia black, both trying for admission to the Junior League," said J.J. Conlin in *Best Sellers*. His conclusion was that "Mead and Baldwin solve nothing and perhaps clarify nothing."

Rap on Race comes off as a noble try, but E.K. Welsh *(Library Journal)* complains of "the idle conversation that takes up too many pages in the book."

Blackberry Winter, more personal, warmer and with some touching passages about her parents and paternal grandmother, is a much more likable work, though to some it sounded as if she dictated it into a tape recorder while waiting for planes in airports throughout the world. The poignant moments are offset by much tangled chronology and unfulfilled descriptions. E.G. Detlefsen *(Library Journal)* typifies the general reaction by liking her behind-the-scenes material about her early expeditions and her attempts to relate her own childhood to present-day problems. But— "Mead has a tendency to be a bit 'preachy' in her chapter on childraising."

One of her lesser-known works, *Twentieth Century Faith*, in which she puts forward her religious beliefs (she remains a practicing Episcopalian), is attacked because she had merely brought together a lot of old articles and essays without revising them—"papers of highly uneven quality," says the noted Protestant theologian Martin Marty in *The Critic*;

he also complains about her "clichés about global culture." Her tribute to Ruth Benedict, *An Anthropologist at Work*, receives something of a similar complaint—it is a "paste-up memorial." The reviewers think she used her essay about her old friend to fight long-forgotten academic battles, and has also not selected the best of Dr. Benedict's works for reprinting.

One gets the idea that Mead is by now not writing books but merely issuing compilations to satisfy a public already attracted by her early works. Surely none of her recent works, it seems, is done with the style and intensity and skill of her first two books.

She seems to do better with her *Redbook* columns, which begin in 1961. It is in these columns that one gets an idea of the themes that run through her mind. Someone asked me about her "philosophy." I could think of none except grandmotherliness, a concern that the world run rightly (according to her own ideas), and that everyone work toward the great Global Village. It is in *Redbook*, in which she speaks to women directly, her calm, rather rambling exhortations to understanding and future cooperation sandwiched amid articles about the new women's sexuality, crash diets and gourmet dinners, shortcuts to redecorating and going it alone, that one finds Mead at her most natural.

Her mind spans all subjects, and she is concerned about everything. Nothing seems to be beyond fixing, at least for her. She is above all an optimist. "Certainly there seem to be grounds for pessimism," she admits about the world, but another column puts down this idea with a firm foot, for, as she constantly emphasizes, "We are in the process of creating a new civilization." There will be problems along the way, especially since others do not think with her clarity, but we will reach this almost heavenly vision, just as certainly as the primitive tribes of the South Pacific thought that someday their islands would flip over, drop the whites into the sea and right themselves, with a golden age for the Melanesians.

Or she may ask rhetorically, "Someday will the whole world be a city?" We know she thinks yes. And for the future Global Village we need a new language, she states firmly. But it won't be English, now so widely spoken; for our shared civilization the secondary tongue should be "the natural language of a small, politically unimportant non-European literate people." This is a tall order, and she avoids giving specific suggestions.

The present world and the coming one share problems, Mead points out, not only that of communication but especially of population, which must be controlled. But we can succeed, she decides, after a sobering analysis of the baby boom, by "free access to information"—that is, to birth control—and "a new shared ethic."

Yet not all is presented on a broad scale. She can speak directly, as if at a coffee klatch, to American women about what it is like to be a guest in a primitive culture, saying in effect, "You can do it too, despite the problems." She says to her readers that "the Arapesh, for instance, were reluctant hosts and guests," and in the Sepik River villages not only an outsider like a trader but even a clan member "used to go in fear of his life." Even in the Manus village today (this is written after a third trip to the Admiralties) "there is no comfortable place for a stranger to stay." On the other hand, "the visitor to Samoa is always welcomed and feasted." And she can pointedly remind her audience that "even the escapists among us, the ones who feel that civilization is dull and confining, are likely to choose a primitive people whose way of life includes the use of soap, cloth, starch, scissors, sewing machines, razors and modern cosmetics." She can talk about the peoples of the South Seas as if everyone now knows about them, and to some extent, everyone does, due to her own travels and books.

Nothing, no matter how seemingly insignificant, escapes her notice and avoids being used to make some kind of point. She can talk of what snapshots mean to a family to recall pleasant times, or how Christmas and the Western New Year have become universal holidays. She can connect the four-teenth-century Portuguese explorer Prince Henry the Navi-gator to the American astronauts as equally brave and daring men adventuring into the unknown. Everything fits into her grand view of the world, of the cosmos, as one vast global society coming into being, made up of parts and pieces of thousands of smaller societies whose children all, almost as one child, have leaped through the invisible but very real time zone demarcated by the first atomic bombs exploded in 1945.

The 1960's are a time of special importance for her, be-cause it is in this period, troubled by the Vietnamese War, campus riots, the growing use of drugs and the flaring inde-pendence of the young, that she comes out squarely in sup-port of the new generations, without alienating too many of the older generations; her streams of consciousness impris-oned in *Redbook*'s pages surely helped quiet some of the fears of parents and grandparents.

In one of her earliest columns she points out that "today's children are the first generation to grow up in a world that has the power to destroy itself." Three years later, in 1965, she emphasizes that the youth riots that are sweeping the world are not the youthful pranks of the past but something else entirely, caused by many new factors, and that adults must share a large part of the blame.

"Large-scale youthful rioting cannot succeed without adult provocation and connivance." Adults have made frightful conditions in the world, she says. "Present-day youthful riot-ing is essentially a drama, a dramatic expression of the tensions within the individual who, wherever he may be, feels hemmed in and powerless to move or get his hand on the reins. . . . With one voice we urge young people to assert themselves, however meaninglessly, while with another voice we tell them—and ourselves—that the performance is carried out in vain." But in another column she can express the idea that youth ought to shape up: that one of the best things for all of them would be a period of national service, good for the nation and the individual alike.

So she goes on, to talk about city planning, gypsies, trial marriages—she thinks a temporary marriage ought to be attempted before a formal marriage is agreed upon, but reader reaction makes her revise her opinions—birth control, the American family, the nature of the policeman (whether he seems fearful or friendly), small-town neighborliness, the space program, nudism (she seems to be in favor of some nudity but is actually ambiguous about it), aggressive behavior, and so on, all in an easy, informative, conversational manner. She is rarely caustic or sarcastic, but from time to time she can take a swipe at the American family. Its plastic, artificial qualities bother Mead, after her experiences in the South Pacific. One of her favorite targets is the American male, and her views of this unfortunate creature deserve a direct quotation.

What does the American man expect in a wife? Probably more than has been expected by any other husband in history. If the American wife fulfills his hopes, however, her rewards are supposed to be great. . . . Her husband will try to come home every evening and never go out on the town with his friends. He will spend his nights in strange cities telephoning to her. He will try never to accept an invitation or take a vacation that doesn't include her. He will carry the biggest life-insurance policy he can afford. He will help every evening and on week-ends, even with a newborn baby. He will carry all her heavy packages. He will try to remember to bring her flowers and small presents and never to give her cause for serious jealousy. . . . He will, in short, be one of the most devoted husbands the world has ever seen—mass-produced by the thousands and safely indistinguishable from every other husband.

That was written in 1962, a period of relative quiet—a few articles, a few seminars, no books. But a year later she is involved in another great project, grander than any she had ever attempted before. Theodore Schwartz, her assistant on the second trip to Manus, proposes a return to the Admi-ralties, his object being a survey of the twenty different languages spoken in the group. She plans an extended ex-pedition. Even by the painstaking standards of current field-work, it is a detailed, ambitious program.

Mead, who is now sixty-two, an age when many elderly Americans are taking early Social Security benefits, lays out a three-year program, during which she will make three visits to the South Pacific. The field trip will culminate in a TV program shot by a National Educational Television crew, filming the ways in which this tiny Melanesian world on Manus has rejected its past to become a part of her Global Village.

"I live neck deep in the past," Mead announces when she arrives at Peré in 1964. Again she has a house to herself; Schwartz, with his new wife Lola, is next door in another house. She finds that one of the children who had worked for her as a houseboy in 1928 has come to reminisce about the past. He is Lokus (formerly Loponiu), and he is about thirteen years younger than she, but "I feel him as frail and old and his hearing and eyesight are going."

Theodore Schwartz

In 1964, in the great central square of the new Peré on Manus, Margaret Mead, accompanied by the inevitable crowd of inquisitive children, stops to make notes. By the time of this trip to Manus, Mead's third, she is accepted as a member of the village and is treated like one of the respected elders.

The entire Manus society is still changing together. It has not been merely a breaking away by one generation, the young, as happened in the West, but an entire people, young, old, middle-aged, men and women, who as a tribe decided to modernize. People who before the war would never have dared sail too far from the sight of land or from the known currents and wave swells, or at night, are now flying in jets.

Dozens of the young people are abroad studying or teaching or holding government posts. Paliau, who was responsible for the new Manus, is now a respected figure at Port Moresby, the new capital of the New Guinea territories. More people are taking Western names, and a new word—"worried"—has crept into the language.

The village itself is open to the outside world. Some houses have rooms set aside with a table, chairs, a bed (the Manus sleep on the floor). Pictures of rock stars hang on the walls: The Beatles, Dylan, the Stones and Baez are no more foreign to the young Manus than they are to young Americans. But there are also changes people don't like to see. Pokanau is growing old, though he is still known as the wise man of the village. He is the one who remembers the warring past, and today he is anxious that his knowledge be taken down on tape so that the Manus of the future will know their history. His sight is failing, but he can still see faraway stars. All his contemporaries have died. In the distant past it was a rare individual who saw the birth of a son's children. Now Pokanau has witnessed the birth of twin great-granddaughters.

The drama of independence, enacted all over the world, from Indonesia to India and Pakistan to Africa and the Pacific islands, is being symbolized in Manus. What was once rebellious and subversive is now legalized, honored.

Mead can now note that Manus is a model for what is happening in the great Global Village, for good and bad. She approves of searching for new knowledge, education and foreign experience, of the desire to participate in world affairs, for the Manus have a strong sense of their own worth. But she can also worry over some of the effects of participation in the world outside.

Paliau, like some others, suffers from "modernization." She notes that he is a member of the New Guinea Parliament, which is working toward statehood, and in 1966 during her stay he is elected president of the Manus Council. Though Paliau might be a political genius, and largely responsible for the progress at Manus, his role is being undermined by lesser men and women. His progress is compromised by his poor English, and the world is being run with English as the lingua franca. Other, younger New Guineans, better educated, fluent in English, challenge him, threaten his leadership. Without English a man cannot communicate with the tribe on the adjoining islands or on the other side of the mountain. Mead sees that Paliau is handicapped even though his integration of the Admiralty Archipelago stands as a monument to his organizing ability.

Still Mead is pleased at the progress she sees. In the council halls at Peré and Port Moresby young people trained as teachers, nurses, clerks, interpreters, accountants and government workers are taking their places in the new government. As happens in virtually every society where there has been a revolution, violent or peaceful, there comes a time, a generation or two later, when the young take over from the Old Guard.

If the Manus were capable of such major changes, what might have happened to the Iatmul? It is a question that interests Mead. Her fellow anthropologist Rhoda Métraux spends a year in planning a trip to the Sepik to investigate the Iatmul at Tambunam, where Bateson and Mead had worked in 1938. What had been heard about Tambunam was not encouraging. During World War II the men's ceremonial house had been bombed. In early 1967 floods temporarily wiped out many gardens and destroyed innumerable coconut trees. Curio hunters were looting the people of their ancient heritage of sacred objects, the masks, drums and carvings that were the sanctified tools of their worship. Moreover, how did the younger people, now being educated in the newly founded schools, react to their head-hunting, war-loving elders, with their endless ceremonies and obscure rituals? Was there anything left to honor? Or had all been swept away by the war and the subsequent leveling of primitive culture by the West?

"I felt rather as if I were hurrying to a deathbed," Mead writes, "to record the death pangs of the Tambunams, once the fiercest, the proudest and most flamboyant people on the Sepik."

The motor launch winds its way up the gently flowing, muddy river to Tambunam. "But I need not have been fearful," Mead reports shortly after her arrival in June 1967. The great houses, with their tremendous carved posts, high pitched roofs, gables and statued eaves are still standing. No longer able to engage in war and head-hunting—the white administration was quite firm about stamping out such practices—the men have experienced a tremendous outburst of creative carving. They have retained what they needed of the past, what was important artistically, and at the same time have selected what is useful in the present, the outboard motors, transistor radios on which they could hear broadcasts from all over New Guinea—especially of music—cigarette lighters, watches and clothing. The school children are dressed in European clothing.

These changes mean a radical transformation in the economic system. Now a European form of currency has replaced shells and dogs' teeth in exchanges. And money means

Back in Tambunam among the Iatmul in 1967, Margaret Mead confers with her principle informants, Mbaan (left) and Peter Mbetnda (right). Mbaan is an authority on tradition and language; Mbetnda, Mead's table boy on her first trip in 1938, is years later a respected and knowledgeable leader in the village.

that men either have to work as laborers or must produce objects which will bring cash rather than barter.

Rhoda Métraux, Mead's long-time collaborator and close friend, has worked with her on many other projects over the years. Métraux is an expert on Haiti and Montserrat in the West Indies. Now she is following up Gregory Bateson's 1930's work with three trips among the "new" Iatmul.

The culture is now a mixed one. The scene has changed little, however. The brown water of the Sepik flows gently or swiftly, according to the season. Across from the great houses, on the opposite bank, are the gardens, and beyond them, stretching to the horizon, are the endless marshes. The people still paddle about in their slender dugout canoes with carved crocodile prows. The newly constructed houses are exactly like the ones built sixty years earlier, when the white man was but a shadow in far-off jungles. Tambunam is still known as the handsomest village on the Sepik.

But changes are noticeable, too. As always, the little children run about naked, but now the older ones wear nylon shirts or blouses, and trousers or dirndl skirts. Many have watches and transistor radios. But like their mothers and grandmothers, the teenage girls still smoke pipes and chew the red-staining betel nut. There is a further, significant change: The Sepik is at peace. No longer is Tambunam, or any of the other villages, threatened by raiding parties from neighboring tribes. Head-hunting is a distant memory, and women are no longer captured and taken off as booty.

There is a joyful reunion, Mead and the villagers, the recollections of each other, of who is dead and who alive, of gossip and memories. Almost immediately Mead and Métraux are asked an unexpected question: Do they have a tape recorder? The Iatmul want their heritage taken down for posterity. So every evening the people come to sing, to chant the old, old war songs and ceremonial rituals and to play their bamboo instruments and drums, listening to what they have just recorded, praising, analyzing and criticizing. The Iatmul have a new stage for their beloved expression of the dramatic.

A man who remembers the past in vivid terms announces, "I will now sing the song we used to sing when the heads of the slain were lined up in the men's house." And after the last soft, haunting notes have died away, enshrined in the plastic tape that makes no judgments, he remarks casually, "Yes, my youngest son is away at school. He is studying to be a doctor."

The Tambunam see not only the old ways within themselves, but the new as well. They can encompass both, without destroying their heritage. They see before them a larger world, of which they and their past are a part, but a world in which they hope their children's future will be different from their own. The older generation lacks the skills for the world beyond the Sepik. But their children, now learning to read and write, will have other opportunities. A villager who spans both generations, the man who brought the first of the Tambunam to their new school, talks to Métraux of the day when "all men, black men and white men, will walk along one road together, sit down together and eat together like brothers."

Despite the continuity of the past that she can see in the Manus and Iatmul, Mead dares not hope for a continuity in her own life. She fears that her inability to bear children easily will be repeated in her daughter, Cathy. In 1960 Cathy marries a young engineer, Barkev Kassarjian, of Armenian ancestry. Like her mother, Cathy wants to combine a career with motherhood.

Mead is concerned about the marriage—perhaps even about marriage as an institution, with three abortive ones behind her. She says, perhaps with Reo in mind, that she rather carefully tried not to "think too much about the kind of father my son-in-law would be." Yet because of her own

Margaret Mead's granddaughter, Sevanne Margaret (called Vanni), with her father, Barkev Kasserjian, and her mother Catherine Bateson. Mead is proud to note that "through no act of my own I had become biologically related to a new human being."

experiences with Grandma Mead she wants to be a "resource," though she believes that Cathy should be able to lead her life independently. In 1947, in the last poem she ever published, Mead had told Cathy, then eight:

> That I be not a restless ghost
> Who haunts your footsteps as they pass
>
> . . .
>
> You must be free to take a path
> Whose end I feel no need to know . . .

But clearly Mead does feel a need to know. She is concerned about Cathy's choice of husband, but she accepts the fact that Barkev is Cathy's mate, not hers, and forces her mind to thinking of what this man with the long Armenian heritage means to her fair-haired daughter of English and American parents, the latter also of English ancestry. Mead seems to be revealing an unsuspected bias here, but she states, "It was an added delight, then, to discover that I enjoyed him very much." She can appreciate "his analytical mind, his keen enjoyment of all the concrete details of life, his sensitive regard for persons and lively respect for the nature of things."

Dark-haired, dark-eyed Barkev Kassarjian meets Mead's approval and becomes—in 1960—a member of her family. The Kassarjians' first child, Martin, born while the couple are living in the Philippines, lives only a few hours. At last, however, in 1969, Cathy successfully bears another child, a daughter named Sevanne Margaret, called Vanni. Now Mead can see the continuity of the future. "I suddenly realized that through no act of my own I had become biologically related to a new human being."

The term "biologically related" might seem too coldly scientific to many people but Mead experiences its human joys, too. "As a new grandmother, I began both to relive my own daughter's infancy and to observe the manifestations of temperament in the tiny creature." As with her mother and grandmother, dual roles are still in operation, those of mother and worker. As a grandmother Mead is extra conscientious: She states she experiences none of the freedom from responsibility that grandmothers are supposed to have. It appears that her obligation to be a resource but not an interference is every bit as demanding now as when Cathy was a baby. In summing up, it is both as a scientist and as a woman who has experienced all three of the major roles—child, mother and grandmother—that she can say—plead—that "everyone needs to have access to both grandparents and grandchildren in order to be a full human being." She adds, "Seeing a child as one's grandchild, one can visualize that same child as a grandparent, and with the eyes of another generation one can see other children. . . ."

She is thinking of her own world, with its generation gaps, its hostilities between parents and children, between parents and grandparents, when she says this. But at the same time it applies to what is happening in Manus, for again that microcosm of change is experiencing another upheaval, like the earlier ones, unexpected. Here grandparents and children are being resources to each other, in ways that charm Mead as a human being and thrill her as a scientist. Life in Manus, one sees, is both linear and cyclical: One goes straight in order to return.

The year is now 1975. Mead has made two quick trips to the South Pacific since her extended expeditions of the 1960's, minor jaunts in 1971 and 1973. Another checking-up seems to be in order, requiring some major work. She arrives in the village of Peré in mid-1975. There seems to be a great psychic reward in her repeated visits, something that satisfies her sense of history and confirms her need for "continuity." In a letter home written shortly after her arrival she says:

> I am most conscious of the enormous sense of continuity as I look at old men whom I knew as children and see the grandfathers' faces reflected in their descendents. The shared memories, the shared experiences bind them together in a web that is stronger than the ancestral ghosts they fear if they do not send money and gifts home to parents who put in hard work to rear them.

Nearly half a century has passed since Mead and Reo Fortune visited Manus. Of all the adults living there half a century ago, only the two foreigners, the tiny American and the tempestuous New Zealander, are still alive. Pokanau, the "lawyer man," their best informant and the repository of the tribe's traditions, has recently died, the last Manus to have witnessed the arrival of the strange white couple on the beach at Peré.

A curious turn of events has taken place at Peré, Mead notes. Just as in America many children or grandchildren of immigrants have taken a new interest in the lands their parents left and the culture they so often rejected in an effort to be truly American (even to the extent of anglicizing their names and abandoning customs, religion and foods), so too have the young Manus begun to wonder about their past. No longer are there elders to tell the people how things "were always done," to keep alive the heritage of music, ritual and custom. But, unlike many small societies (and even larger ones) that have made a transition from a primitive world to a modern world, the Manus have a thorough record of the old days. Their past life is excellently described in the popular, still-in-print book, *Growing Up in New Guinea*, and in a number of technical papers (Mead's "Kinship, in the Admiralty

Islands," "An Investigation of the Thought of Primitive Children with Special Reference to Animism," and Fortune's "Manus Religion"), the literature from the 1953 trip (Mead's *New Lives for Old*, Theodore Schwartz's *The Paliau Movement*), and the thousands of photographs, the documentary films, even the drawings done by the children under Mead's persuasion. And then others have also studied the Manus, so there is no lack of information about their past and their recent history.

However, the Manus now have some basic questions they want answered. Have they thrown out too much? Have they gone too far into the modern world? Mead, in her trip to Peré in 1975, is to find a new Manus, one she had expected no more than the one she had found in 1953.

Continued observation of a single culture over an extended period is rare in anthropology. Mead's first return to Manus in 1953 was itself unusual, and her subsequent trips back to the island produced ethnological research unlike anything else ever done. Each voyage since the very beginning has been one of discovery. In 1975 she notes changes that no one could ever have anticipated. For the Manus, having deliberately rejected much of their own culture and systematically accepted Western civilization on a very pragmatic basis, picking and choosing what they thought would work—in a Manus context—now reject parts of the new world and deliberately seek to reintegrate elements of the old Manus culture.

In 1975 the entire area, not only Manus but all the islands within the New Guinea archipelago, has become an independent state, Papua New Guinea. The new nation has been self-governing since September. When Mead stops at Port Moresby, the capital of the new nation, she encounters a number of people from Manus, who, like other members of once-primitive tribal groups, are now holding important positions. One man from Manus is the new chancellor of the University of Papua New Guinea; another Manus man is the minister of housing for the nation; she meets another young Manus who is on his way to the United States to study comparative literature.

On Manus itself, at the new provincial capital of Lorengau, she meets a young poet, the first from Manus; he is teaching creative writing at the local high school. Another young man, who had gone to Chicago to study for the priesthood, has returned home to put his energies into more secular work; he is in charge of dredging a polluted channel.

In the villages there is a practical alliance of old and new. Plywood is being used alongside traditional planks and palm thatch. Such Westernization in daily life is to be expected. What is significant is the return to prewhite traditions.

Ancient Manus customs have resurfaced. The old practice of validating marriages by the exchanges of goods through "the side of the man" and "the side of the woman" has been restored, except that in 1975, in place of sago, fish, pigs, oil and goods traded from other tribes, the exchanges are effected through European goods and gambling winnings in European currency. And where dogs' teeth and shells had been basic to family exchanges at a wedding, now cash alone could be the basis of validation.

Old ceremonies are again being practiced; dances, songs and oratory in the old style have become popular. And the drums, which during the postwar period had been made of cast-off torpedo casings, are again being carved in the ancient slit wooden gong style. And while a woman might wear a Western brassiere but no blouse, she has returned to the traditional multicolored grass skirt, having abandoned the famous Mother Hubbard imposed by missionaries.

Deeper reforms can be observed too. In the late 1920's, when Mead and her husband had first visited the Manus, the young men expressed their new rebelliousness against the control of their elders by going off to work on plantations and refusing to send their wages home. Now the young men, like their fathers and grandfathers, still go away to work but insist that if they send their earnings back to the villages, the money must be wisely invested. And some of the young men who had aspirations to an entirely different way of life and had gone away for education, to the main island of New Guinea or to a foreign country, are now returning home to resume the hereditary ways of trading and fishing, ways which some young people had even despised for a while as being too "native."

A new consciousness has developed in Manus. It is still an integrated society, and just as it has moved into the twentieth century as a unit, it is now moving into its new "true" self as a unit. After she returns home, Mead can remark that she has been fortunate in witnessing a primitive people's emergence out of the bleak, limited milieu of the Stone Age into an almost total absorption in Western ways, and then a final balancing between the best of both. Mead remarks in *Natural History* magazine:

> The extreme emphasis on modernization and rejection of the characteristics of an earlier period were now gone. The society was still distinctively Manus, but with a new sense of identity, ready to combine the old and the new. I realized how little we had been able to learn when we used to study a people only once, and how illuminating and unique was this opportunity to follow the same population—a microcosm of the world—for forty-seven years, as they

fanned out into the wider world, but retained the core of their culture at home.

The Manus are a kind of touchstone for Mead. But she does not limit herself to them, though they are the core of her work, of her deepest thoughts. Planes have made anthropological work easier, and Mead travels constantly, and whatever she sees is with an anthropologist's eye. A visit to Rhoda Métraux in Montserrat in the West Indies in 1966 gives her a quick study of a Caribbean village; a trip to see the Schwartzes, at work in a Mexican village, not only enables her to view Latin American village life in capsule form but to see displaced villagers in Mexico City's slums with the help of Oscar Lewis, who has specialized in that aspect of anthropology. On other trips here and there she can stop off at a desert settlement in Saudi Arabia to note the ways in which nomadic Arabs adapt to their environment, and then spend two weeks at a kibbutz in Israel, make a trip to a reserve for aboriginals in Australia, visit Iran where she observes nomads on a market day. Even when she is forced to make stopovers on long trips she does not waste idle hours in hotels or in shopping: In South Africa, with a few hours to spare, she rushes off to a native village, and in Japan a day in a traditional Japanese village with a Japanese anthropologist gives her more insights into the nature of people and their ways of living. Whatever exists, whatever is, goes into her head, to be stored and retrieved when the proper time comes. Not a moment is wasted: Waiting out a rainy day in Montserrat she reads *Encounter, Counterpart* and *Transaction* magazines, Kenneth Read's *The High Valley* (a book about the highlands of New Guinea), Chow's *Social Mobility in China* and Goveia's *Slave Society in the British Leeward Islands at the End of the Eighteenth Century.*
Mead has an intense memory: She can recall sights,

scents, sounds from her childhood, so she can speak knowingly of what it is like to be a child. She has been in love
and has married men of promise and talent and has been
three times divorced. She suffered the tragedies of miscarriages but had a child, and after her, a grandchild. She has
seen savage lands as well as American suburbs and city
life. She can speak knowingly to people of all ages. Her
immense knowledge and experience, her compassion and
understanding, make it possible for her to talk of what is
shared in common by jungle tribes, highly civilized Balinese, and twentieth-century Westerners. Her interest is
what is held in common, but she is also as aware of what is
diverse and different, and of everyone's right to a very
personal independent life.

All experience seems to fall within her grasp. The cry of a
jungle baby heard in 1930 is as vivid to her as the nighttime
cries of her daughter and granddaughter. The death of old
informants in Samoa is as close as the more recent deaths of
her own parents. All life is awake to her, throbbing to be
heard, and she listens, records, writes, photographs and
speaks. She is absorbed with life, absorbed with the continuity
of life, and absorbed in the ways in which each person works
out his or her life. Certain elements are passed down from
one generation to another, but they also repeat, return, in
order to lend depth to human growth. Patterns, traits, customs, traditions surface again and again to give strength to
life.

Her memory can go back to her grandparents, and beyond
that to what she has been told of *their* grandparents. And now
she is projecting into the future, wondering about granddaughter Vanni's grandchildren. It is a tremendous span of
life and Mead is in the center of it, with her fingers on every
throb of humanity's pulse, her notebooks and tape recorders
and cameras ready to analyze, imprint and remember what

her vast slice of humanity has done and said.

Old age interests her along with birth. Approaching a biblical span of years, she can look at her own lifetime with scientific curiosity and objectivity. She can recall her own angers at her father, her impatience with her mother. But all of these adolescent attitudes are tempered by her recollection of both parents in their last years, as she sees them—almost like a speeded-up film—progress from the active, exciting, involved young couple of her childhood into middle age with its slowing down and the final, almost static years of old age. By the late 1940's she had become aware that they had indeed grown old and that the end was near. "The way in which one's parents grow old matters a great deal," she believes. Her mother, who had a stroke, fought to recover. Her father's personality remained intact and his mind stayed keen and fresh, alert to whatever was new and interesting. Then, in a surprising reassessment of the influences upon her early life, she decides that it was her father, more than her mother or even Grandma Mead, who had been most important, "who defined for me my place in the world."

"Watching a parent grow is one of the most reassuring experiences anyone can have," she says, "a privilege that comes only to those whose parents live beyond their children's early adulthood." Emily Mead died in 1950 but her husband survived her another six years. He continued to develop and mature until the end. Mead remarks that, when she gave a seminar shortly before his death, he, rather than the young people, asked the most searching questions. And she is proud to state that he gave up his earlier racial prejudices and also came to accept such new institutions as Social Security and other social programs which he had once opposed as government interference in private life.

She adds, "I have been fortunate in being able to look up

to my parents' minds well past my middle years." They, too, as well as Grandma Mead, were resources.

As a grandmotherly resource herself and as a scientist, her work goes on. Mead, having served the American Museum of Natural History as a curator of various kinds for forty-two years, is made Curator Emeritus in 1969. The books, articles, reviews continue in profusion. The United States Congress, the United Nations, public and private institutions and organizations and NASA, call on her for advice, seminars, speeches. She is a visiting professor here and there, a consultant in the social sciences, chairwoman and chairperson of numerous organizations and committees, each job or honor alone worth a lifetime of work.

The writer Gail Sheehy (in an article in *New York* magazine) asked how she could fit together so many lives. "You certainly had to make some sacrifices and compromises along the way," said Ms. Sheehy about Mead's combining career and motherhood and doing so much with each.

"Yes," Ms. Sheehy reports her as saying. "Because I have enough energy to do two jobs. For my generation, to have even one child and a career took a tremendous amount of energy. Which I had. . . . And I understand the culture well enough to study and, in a sense, to outwit it."

But Mead is being modest here. It takes a full-time "bibliographer" on her staff to get the facts of her life in order—the trips, the publications, the events, the titles, the positions, the honors—but sorting things out consumes years, and a final compilation is not ready until the winter of 1976, the time of her seventy-fifth birthday. An interviewer at the time calls Mead "an industrious conglomerate." Her assistants—four hard-working young women serving their apprenticeships as anthropologists—refer to her as "the General."

A doctoral candidate at the Massachusetts Institute of

Wherever she goes, Margaret Mead is surrounded by young people eager to hear her encouraging messages on "Growing Up" and "Coming of Age." Here she takes time out from a World Population Conference sponsored by the United Nations to talk to teenage questioners in Bucharest, Romania.

Technology, Rae Goddell, points out that Mead is one of a handful of "visible scientists" who play an extraordinary role in communicating their latest views on important issues, even though the subjects are often outside the scientists' chosen field. Circumventing traditional scientific channels of communication—the technical paper published (or buried) in an academic journal would be one—these scientists go straight to the public with their opinions on such subjects as environment, energy, race and I.Q., war and population. Miss Goddell had examined forty major figures, putting eight in the first rank, one of whom is Mead (the others are Isaac Asimov, Barry Commoner, Paul Ehrlich, Linus Pauling, Glenn Seaborg, William Shockley and B.F. Skinner). A controversial, colorful, issue-oriented figure is her opinion of Mead, as of the others. The public sees the scientists credibly, for they have long-established reputations, and can speak out in language the average person can understand. Thus Mead (as with the other "visible" scientists) is a "resource" for the public, for Americans and for the world, just as she is for Cathy and Vanni.

The Old Turtle

WHAT OF MEAD HERSELF, STILL active in her seventies, still hopping off on trips, after half a century in the Pacific and at home, in which she had combined the old and the new, had crossed rural frontiers into the nuclear, electronic age, had become a member of the Global Village? Now truly an "old turtle"—it is an image she referred to several times in her writings, for it pleased her—she could sum up her career on the celebration of her seventy-fifth birthday with humor and insight.

"Sooner or later I'm going to die," she told Laurie Johnston of *The New York Times,* sounding as if she didn't mean it, for she seemed a lot more durable than the brownstone mass of the Museum where she was speaking, "but I'm not going to retire." She appeared to be indestructible.

The Museum seemed to agree, for it established a Margaret Mead Fund for the Advancement of Anthropology. Some five million dollars are to be raised; she is the key figure in the activities. Five million dollars!—and she went on her first field trip funded by a mere $450 doled out piecemeal. The money will endow a Margaret Mead Chair of Anthropology at the Museum, finance research scholars and help preserve, reorganize and "edit" the Museum's collection, and will reopen the

Hall of the Pacific, which Mead long ago assembled. Almost enough to keep Mead busy, but not quite, for she had her seminars, trips here and there, appearances before august bodies of scientists, academics and legislators, as well as playing a role model—self-sufficient, understanding, noncriticizing, being open and helpful, a resource—for Vanni and thousands of other young people looking for someone in the older generations who knew what it was like to grow up, who could speak in calm terms about adolescence, drugs, education, sex, conflicts with parents, war, the environment, generation gaps, shared futures arising from the dichotomous past.

She maintained a busy schedule, spending less time in her Museum cave, and doing much office work from her apartment on Central Park West, a few blocks from the Museum. She would arise at five, no matter how late she had come home the night before from a trip or a lecture or a rare evening with friends, to go over stacks of mail that she would annotate for her secretaries, skim through magazines and books, sign letters and approve (but rarely reject) applications from students for grants. The entire pile would be stuffed into shopping bags and left outside her door, where one of the assistants would pick it up and take it to the "cave," returning at the end of the day with another pile. The process would be repeated five times a week.

During the day she might drop by the Museum for a short while, or take a plane to Washington, or some other city, for a lecture or a meeting; she liked to return home the same day if possible. Her personal interests seemed to have been reduced to Cathy and Vanni. Her lingering emotions about the three men she had married seemed faint; she was resentful of Reo Fortune, but tolerant of Bateson, with whom she might share a speaking engagement. More often she could be humorous and deprecating about all three. "All my marriages were interesting—they were all endogamous," she said to

Laurie Johnston, explaining for the uninitiated, "That means, 'within the group.' " She had an interesting view of what had happened. "It wasn't so much that they didn't work out—they got used up. They were like theatrical marriages, when the two play opposite each other on a stage."

An interesting view, which might have stood some examination in *Sex and Temperament,* her analysis of South Seas male and female roles.

Her views were always very positive. The world is an active, encouraging place. One sees it with enthusiasm. Growing Up. Coming of Age. A Way of Seeing. New Lives for Old. Growth and Culture.

Positive views. The world is becoming a unit. The Global Village. We have crossed a divide, a watershed in history marked by World War II. The parents, the grandparents came from isolated cultures, unrelated societies. Papa Franz Boas had long ago demolished the belief that society stems from a common origin. Before the watershed all is diverse, after, all is one. The new generations are linked together by music, political ideas, blue jeans, a yearning for freedom, by eight visible scientists. By Margaret Mead.

Often she was asked what she would choose to do if she had her life to live over again.

"About this there is no doubt in my mind. I would elect to be an anthropologist."

Up to the end of her life Mead worked and traveled, advised, wrote, lectured, planned for the future. More trips to the Pacific, always if possible with a stopover at Manus, to see what the people, collectively or alone, had done. No trip was too far, none too esoteric. She visited Cathy and Vanni and son-in-law Barkev in Iran, where they were teaching.

The trip was no more fatiguing than hopping off to Washington to testify before, or lecture to, a congressional committee.

For a long time she relied upon her staff to handle details, work out plans for her. She had seen so much, thought so much, observed so much, analyzed so much, written so much, that in her last years she threw out all but the essential. Her assistants plotted the minutiae of daily life for her, moved her about on her travels, gave her cards each day with schedules. Her mind was on other things. She might claim from time to time that her memory was failing, but she seemed to have total recall for every fall of a leaf in the jungle, every nuance of faces from Museum halls to Bali. The problem may have been that in her seventies she suffered from information overload, like an overworked computer that has been programmed with too many details of primitive, advanced and industrial societies, languages, ways of sitting, speaking, dancing, forms of etiquette in addressing tribal chiefs and heads of state. Too much to remember, perhaps.

She was one of the great figures on our horizon, tying the rites and rituals of Stone Age ex-cannibals to the rites and rituals of technological men and women, seeing the common humanity in all, envisioning a shared future for the slim brown-skinned children of Manus and the Sepik and the white-skinned children of the West, communicating not only through English (which they all seemed to be learning now) but through rock and funk, blue jeans and *Mad,* wall posters and transistors.

To the end, the old turtle, crossing the seas of the world by jet, by canoe, here and there, Manus, Iran, Bali, the Sepik, India, London, Africa, to wherever there was work to do, something to note, something to say, an observation to record. The death drums beat too early. When they sounded again, the deep rumble could only have been an echo.

"Sooner or later I'm going to die," Mead had said. Had she a forewarning of the terrible, sudden cancer that was to strike her down? She seemed indestructible, enduring, a rock. An institution. More permanent than the massive Museum walls that were her home. I wrote this book while Mead was still alive, travelling, lecturing, talking, speaking out, giving opinions and pronouncements, spanning generations and continents alike with formidable ease. The death of the great, as well as of relative and friend, often may come as a personal blow. I had lived with this biographical portrait a long time, from the moment that I had realized that Margaret Mead would be an interesting subject for a book—I had been doing research for a trip to the South Pacific, where I studied a Cargo Cult in the New Hebrides similar to the one that Paliau had initiated in Manus. I could see Mead's greatnesses, and some of her faults. The latter I often overlooked: This is a book not about her lapses but her successes. In retrospect I think she was not an easy person. She stood too far above the heads of others to bend. She had talents that most of us lack. She could see from a distance, a grand view with a 360° arc; at the same time she could discover microscopic significant details that linked cultures, civilizations, families, races, tribes, communities and nations. Close up with people she could be very difficult; some of her personal relationships ended in disaster. A few of her friends had remarked that she never, or rarely, had to suffer the private torments that many people experience, and that she was unable to understand that sometimes situations and circumstances overpower lesser mortals. Mead conquered where others succumbed. Moreover, she was blessed with good fortune and success: She always could draw upon the money and resources for her work; she was never denied funds for a project or an expedition, while other workers languished because they were unable to obtain financing in order to undertake valuable projects. Mead seemed to have little need of monetary rewards; her rewards came in the form of public recognition, though academic approval was never as great as might have been expected. Her formidable talents brought much opposition from her less gifted peers. Yet I am sure it was Margaret Mead, taking off from the foundations laid by Franz Boas and Ruth Benedict, who changed anthropology from a minor and neglected science into the popular subject it has become.

In writing the early chapters I felt that the role of her husbands in her success has been underplayed. She was married to two exceptional men during a crucial period in her career, in her twenties and thirties, an age when the basis for great reputations is founded. Both Reo Fortune and Gregory Bateson have never received as much recognition as I think they deserved for their part in Mead's life. Personally, I liked that eccentric, sometimes abrasive, character, Reo Fortune, and people who read the manuscript of the book have commented on it. Mead, carrying on age-old arguments, disliked my sympathies for him when she was shown the text before it went into production; Bateson, too, whose range and scope of interests surpassed Fortune's, is an amazing and talented figure who deserves wider credit and fame.

Mead was fortunate in the breadth of her life, which included a vanishing rural America and the technological space age, the most primitive of archaic societies and the most advanced of the modern. No one, I think, has been so articulate in binding such disparate cultures into one global view.

In the vast hall of her home base, The American Museum of Natural History, Margaret Mead poses for photographer Ken Heyman with her New Guinea forked stick, a symbol of authority. The stick, which she always carries in her later years, has come to be a kind of primitive magic for Mead.

Selected Bibliography

MARGARET MEAD HAS BEEN AN extremely prolific writer, but it was not until 1976 that a complete bibliography of her works was drawn up. Though she has some eighteen "popular" books to her credit, many of her writings are highly technical and beyond the scope of the average reader; most of her papers appeared in academic journals with extremely limited circulations, and are virtually impossible to locate outside a specialized library. However, most of her books written for the general public are kept in print in various hardcover and paperback editions, and can usually be found in good libraries and bookstores. Some works, like *Coming of Age in Samoa* and *Growing Up in New Guinea*, have been reprinted in so many editions that it is difficult to know which are in print at the moment. Others of her books are less widely reprinted.

Though Mead is a national, even international, figure, there is little writing about her, except for reviews of her books, critiques in academic journals, and a few popular articles. The primary sources for her life are her own works, especially *Blackberry Winter* and *Letters from the Field 1925–1975*. *Blackberry Winter* is available in both hardcover (Morrow) and paperback (Simon & Schuster) editions. The autobiography covers the years of her life up to World War II, with some afterthoughts about her daughter Cathy and granddaughter Vanni. There are many memorable passages about her parents and the continuity she sees in her own child and grandchild, but some of the material is hastily written, as if she were dictating on the run. *Letters from the Field*, also available in both hardcover and paperback (Harper & Row), fills out with much humor and detailed information and local color what is only sketched in the autobiographical accounts of the field trips.

Mead's first two books, *Coming of Age in Samoa* and *Growing Up in New Guinea*, are definitely her best and should be read. The first title is the one that made her famous and helped make the profession of the anthropologist both glamorous and respectable. *Growing Up in New Guinea* is her account of the Manus whom she visited in 1928 (and did not expect to see again). It should be read with *New Lives for Old*, the work in which she tells what happened to the tribe in the twenty-five years after her first field trip to their island. Unfortunately, the follow-up work lacks the conciseness and vividness of the initial work, though the material is far more dramatic, since it deals with a people who have rejected the past, survived a major war and deliberately moved into the modern world.

Two works deal with her favorite subject, the differences between male and female and what causes them. They are *Sex and Temperament in Three Primitive Societies* and *Male and Female: A Study of the Sexes in a Changing World*. The first title analyzes sexual types among men and women as she saw them among the Arapesh, the Mundugumor and the Tchambuli; the latter includes these tribes and a number of other societies, including American. Both works seem highly subjective, some points get lost and several conclusions are not clear.

A Way of Seeing is a collection of her wide-ranging columns from *Redbook* magazine. Here she is at her most grandmotherly, but she is also calm and often makes it seem that her viewpoint is the right one, which it may be at times. *A Rap on Race* is the famous dialogue with the black writer James Baldwin; many well-expressed personal viewpoints but also much irrelevant material that gets in the way of the discussion.

THE HUSBANDS' WORKS

Margaret Mead's second and third husbands, Reo F. Fortune and Gregory Bateson, are both superlative anthropologists, perceptive, concise, imaginative, but not so visible to the world as she was. The books they did on field trips shared with her, or on related subjects, are worth reading, though they are harder going than Mead's work. Fortune's *Sorcerers of Dobu*, about the very formidable and dour magicians of Dobu, should be read along with her *Growing Up in New Guinea*, though it is often difficult to understand, since Reo does not compromise either with himself or the reader. Mead's *The Changing Culture of an Indian Tribe*, about her field trip to the Omaha reservation, should be accompanied by Fortune's *Omaha Secret Societies*, for they are a good example of how two scientists can see the same situation in different terms.

Bateson's *Naven* forms a trilogy with *Growing Up in New Guinea* and *Sorcerers of Dobu* in its picture of primitive societies in the Southwest Pacific. It is, like Fortune's book, a complex work and not easily finished, making many demands upon the reader. Bateson gets the major credit for *Balinese*

Character, the photo study of Bali done with Mead. The photographs are interesting but not unusual, despite Mead's pride in developing a "new" technique of presenting ideas and themes visually.

This has been a rather personal bibliography. Many of Mead's other works are available but, to many readers, of limited interest. Among them are: *And Keep Your Powder Dry* (1942), *Soviet Attitudes Toward Authority* (1951), *The Small Conference* (1968), *Culture and Commitment* (1970), *Twentieth Century Faith* (1972) and *Ruth Benedict* (1974), to list a few. Then there is Mead's favorite work, *Continuities in Cultural Evolution.*

Few books are written in isolation. I owe great debts of gratitude to my editors, Edite Kroll and Robert O. Warren of Harper & Row; to Dina S. Guha of Bombay (where the manuscript was begun); to Christopher H. Rice for some basic anthropological texts; to the staff of the Hampton Library for finding certain rare works; to Amy Bard, a member of Dr. Mead's staff; and especially to Dr. Rhoda Métraux, who twice went over the text with much patience.

Index

Designed by Kohar Alexanian
Set in 11 pt Gael
Composed by The Haddon Craftsmen, Inc.
Printed and bound by The Murray Printing Company
HARPER & ROW PUBLISHERS, INC.